THE DEVIL TAKES BITCOIN

Jake Adelstein has been an investigative journalist in Japan since 1993, writing in Japanese and English. He authored *Tokyo Vice* (now an HBO series), *The Last Yakuza* (2023), and *Tokyo Noir* (2024), and co-hosted the award-winning podcast *The Evaporated: Gone with the Gods*. A recognised expert on Japan's organised crime, he has reported for *The Daily Beast*, *Los Angeles Times*, *Tempura*, and *VICE*. He is also a low-ranking Zen Buddhist priest, trying hard to be kinder and occasionally exorcising hungry ghosts. Adelstein frequently appears as a commentator on Japanese crime and culture, working as a writer and consultant.

THE DEVIL TAKES BITCOIN

CRYPTOCURRENCY CRIMES AND THE JAPANESE CONNECTION

JAKE ADELSTEIN
with NATHALIE STUCKY

SCRIBE

Melbourne | London | Minneapolis

Scribe Publications
18–20 Edward St, Brunswick, Victoria 3056, Australia
2 John St, Clerkenwell, London, WC1N 2ES, United Kingdom
3754 Pleasant Ave, Suite 223w, Minneapolis, Minnesota 55409, USA

Originally published as *J'ai vendu mon âme en Bitcoins*
Copyright © Editions Marchialy, Groupe Delcourt, 2019

This updated edition published by Scribe in 2025
Copyright © Jake Adelstein 2019, 2025

The publisher expressly prohibits the use of *The Devil Takes Bitcoin* in connection with the development of any software program, including, without limitation, training a machine-learning or generative artificial intelligence (AI) system.

All rights reserved, including those for text and data mining, AI training, and similar technologies. Without limiting the rights under copyright reserved above, no part of this publication may be reproduced, stored in or introduced into a retrieval system, or transmitted, in any form or by any means (electronic, mechanical, photocopying, recording or otherwise) without the prior written permission of the publishers of this book.

The moral rights of the author have been asserted.

Typeset in 12/17 pt Fairfield Light by the publishers

Printed and bound in the UK by CPI Group (UK) Ltd,
Croydon CR0 4YY

Scribe is committed to the sustainable use of natural resources and the use of paper products made responsibly from those resources.

978 1 761381 30 0 (Australian edition)
978 1 917189 24 8 (UK edition)
978 1 964992 17 4 (US edition)
978 1 761386 30 5 (ebook)

Catalogue records for this book are available from the
National Library of Australia and the British Library.

scribepublications.com.au
scribepublications.co.uk
scribepublications.com

To Christopher Dickey (1951–2020), RIP. An incredible editor, journalist, and mentor;

Nathalie-Kyoko Stucky, who helped write the first draft;

Amy Yoshida-Plambeck, who helped complete and write the new edition;

Tigran Gambaryan, a stellar special agent and hero; and

Satoshi Nakamoto, who made this book possible and owes me $100,000,000 in fiat currency, or at least a pizza.

CONTENTS

Introduction	1
Prologue	9
ONE: Meet Magical Tux	17
TWO: Searching for Satoshi Nakamoto	31
THREE: The magical Mt. Gox	59
FOUR: Down dark roads of silk and cyberspace	71
FIVE: The rise and rise of Mt. Gox	81
SIX: Crime pays ... if you're getting paid in bitcoins	93
SEVEN: The Ides of February	115
EIGHT: The unusual suspects	135
NINE: And justice for none	149
TEN: What really happened	165
Epilogue	189
Acknowledgments	209

Introduction

Saint Paul never said that money was the root of all evil; he said it was the *love* of money that was the root of all evil. But when it comes to cryptocurrency—especially Bitcoin—I'm not so sure that there isn't something inherent in this digital gold itself that draws out the worst in people.

In 2014, when I first began covering bitcoin for *The Daily Beast*, cryptocurrency was still a novelty, and the world's largest bitcoin exchange was run out of a small office in downtown Tokyo. Eleven years later, it's a colossal industry, with cryptocurrency being blamed for destabilizing the national fiat currency of some countries, and companies like Binance and others controlling billions of dollars in transactions a day.

We can't deny the amazing power of money—or moolah, loot, lucre, among all the various words we have for it. In Japan, people are certainly aware of that power. There's a saying that I am quite fond of, *Jigoku no sata mo kane shidai*, which you could translate as "Even at the gates of hell, it just depends on how much money you have."

At the risk of sounding insensitive, 2008 was a great year for me. On October 14, my nemesis and a public enemy, Tadamasa Goto—one of the most ruthless yakuza in Japan—was banished from gangster life and forced to live out his days as a civilian. It was the beginning of the end for him.

It was also the year when Bitcoin began. It all began with a mysterious figure named Satoshi Nakamoto. In 2008, Nakamoto published a white paper titled "Bitcoin: A Peer-to-Peer Electronic Cash System," and in doing so, gave birth to what would become a multi-trillion-dollar phenomenon. To this day, no one knows who Satoshi Nakamoto is—whether he's one person, a group of people, or even just a particularly clever form of AI (although, for him to be AI in 2008 would be quite a feat, and an unlikely one). He wrote his white paper, mined the first bitcoins, and corresponded with early adopters, then disappeared into the ether in 2014. Since then, Satoshi has become more of a myth than a man—a digital ghost whose vision for an independent, decentralized currency took on a life of its own.

It's hard to know exactly when the world became obsessed with bitcoin, but if you had to pick a moment, the October 1, 2011 publication of "The Underground Website Where You Can Buy Any Drug Imaginable" by Adrian Chen could be one of them. The article let everyone know there was a place where you could buy drugs right off the web—albeit the dark web—as easily as buying old jeans on eBay. And, what's more, you could buy it with an untraceable (so it was thought) new kind of virtual currency. In an email exchange, Satoshi Nakamoto casually mentioned that one of Bitcoin's potential uses was to buy things you'd rather keep private. Specifically, he suggested it could be used to purchase "porn" without your wife knowing.

Well, he was only a little off when he suggested porn being the commodity that would spark widespread use of his cryptocurrency; it turned out that drugs—legal and illegal—were what people really wanted to buy with Bitcoin.

However, if you were looking for more milestones in the history of Bitcoin, February 2014 wouldn't be a bad guess, either. That was when Mt. Gox, a massive Tokyo-based Bitcoin exchange, started to fall apart. Picture this: a ragtag band of journalists, cryptocurrency fanatics, and confused investors, all orbiting around the disintegrating black hole that was Mt. Gox. The exchange was imploding, and, with it, so was half a billion dollars of digital assets. For a brief moment, it seemed like the experiment called Bitcoin was about to be written off as yet another quirky, misguided tech venture. You know, like those Segway tours you see weaving through public parks—earnest but ultimately laughable.

I should also point out that the inventor of Segway, while riding one of his bikes, ran off a cliff and fell to his death. He's definitely, definitely dead. Satoshi Nakamoto? No one knows.

The death of Bitcoin has been proclaimed many times. But Bitcoin, like a semi-sentient zombie, has always had other plans. When Mt. Gox collapsed, it was supposed to be the end of cryptocurrency, or at least its sobering moment of reckoning. And yet, it turned out to be more like the Big Bang: chaotic, but also the start of something far larger. The implosion of Mt. Gox, once the giant of all Bitcoin exchanges, did what any good disaster does: it sparked curiosity, it lured opportunists, and it shifted something fundamental in how we thought about value. Cryptocurrency picked itself up, dusted itself off, and grew.

I think of Mt. Gox now as a tragicomic prelude to what came next, and how it ultimately changed the economy, much like how a bad dinner date can eventually lead to a happy marriage—just not in any way you expected. The rise and fall of Mark Karpelès, the Frenchman-turned-Tokyo resident at the center of the exchange's implosion, was a spectacle. He was a character you couldn't help but watch, like a magician who knows the trick is failing but somehow hopes he'll still pull it off. He believed that Mt. Gox was more than just a trading platform; it was supposed to be the conduit for a global economic shift, a way to liberate money from the grubby fingers of bankers and regulators. And while Mt. Gox did indeed collapse under its own mismanagement and scandal, Bitcoin itself didn't die—it flourished. People simply couldn't resist the allure of an unregulated, decentralized currency that spoke to the anarchist, libertarian, and get-rich-quick schemer in all of us.

What followed was an explosion of exchanges, innovations, and, yes, a good number of scams. There was Coincheck in Japan, where, in 2018, half a billion dollars disappeared in another hack—a saga eerily reminiscent of Mt. Gox. Except, this time, it didn't feel like the end of the world. By then, the cryptosphere was bigger, more chaotic, and, ironically, more resilient. When Mt. Gox went down, people called it a tragedy. By the time Coincheck got hacked, it was just Tuesday.

If you think about it, cryptocurrency's post-2014 rise is as much a testament to our boundless capacity for hope as it is to our knack for forgetting past mistakes. Bitcoin became the first cryptocurrency to hit the scene, but it was certainly not the last. New cryptocurrencies began cropping up, each promising something that Bitcoin couldn't quite deliver: faster transactions, more privacy, or just a chance to ride the next wave. Ethereum came along, and decided it wasn't enough to be just a currency; it had to be a platform. A way to create decentralized applications, a kind of global computer, if you will. Then there were altcoins such as Ripple and Litecoin, and the tongue-in-cheek Dogecoin—fancy ways of saying "Bitcoin, but different." As the criminals of the world began to realize that you can actually trace Bitcoin, they moved to Monero, the ultimate anonymous currency. It's now so strongly associated with criminal activity that legitimate cryptocurrency exchanges refuse to even list it, much less deal in it.

Inevitably, in order to be the next best thing, companies began making promises that were too good to be true. The downfall of FTX (once the third-largest cryptocurrency exchange by volume) and the collapse of their native tokens (now known to be not much more than a book-cooking instrument) in 2022 is the most blatant recent example. Founder Sam Bankman-Fried—SBF, to those who insist on making lame things cool via acronyms— was heavily tattled on by his executive team and former colleagues, and was very publicly convicted of fraud and money laundering, among other things.

Of course, the scale of the FTX collapse dwarfs what happened at Mt. Gox, the granddaddy of all crypto disasters.

But in Mt Gox's case, it was much less clear-cut as to whether their downfall was due to company malfeasance or something else entirely. (Which is what this book is about, unless you cheat and Google the conclusion.)

I remember talking to some early Bitcoin adopters back in those days, and they were all believers, but not necessarily in the same thing. Some believed in the philosophy, the idea that this was going to unshackle money from the clutches of the state. Others just believed in getting rich. And, it turns out, it didn't really matter what they believed, as long as they bought in. And buy in they did—right up to the point that the price of a single Bitcoin touched $20,000, far exceeding by extension the $450 million that vanished into the ether from Mt. Gox. If that moment in 2017 taught us anything, it's that people's appetite for risk and reward is insatiable, and maybe just a little delusional.

In a way, it was the collapse of Mt. Gox that gave Bitcoin its mythic stature. The way it survived that disaster gave people faith, as if cryptocurrency were some kind of phoenix. When things are too easy, we get bored. Bitcoin's early near-death experiences gave it grit, made it something more than just code. And even as Mark Karpelès himself was being hauled off in Japan—dressed in a Monokuma cap, no less—the price of Bitcoin eventually surged. It's almost poetic, in a way, that the very collapse that threatened the currency was what legitimized it in the eyes of so many. Nothing says "value" quite like surviving an existential crisis.

Of course, we also saw the birth of blockchain evangelists, people who looked at Bitcoin and decided it wasn't just about money. They began to talk about "trustless systems" and "smart contracts"—concepts that seemed to promise a better, more democratic version of nearly everything. They told us that blockchain was going to change how we do business, how we vote, and maybe even how we fall in love (though that last one hasn't quite taken off). The language they used was often as opaque as the code itself, but the message was clear: this was the future.

Cryptocurrency didn't just evolve; it spread like a contagion, jumping from the geeky fringes into the mainstream. Once it was no longer about whether Bitcoin would survive, but rather about which billionaire was buying it, you knew it had arrived. Suddenly, people were talking about Bitcoin on cable news, politicians were debating how to regulate it, and every Uber driver had a theory on when to "buy the dip." Somewhere along the line, Bitcoin stopped being a niche obsession and became a barometer of our collective hope—or our folly.

And here we are in 2025, with cryptocurrencies now an economy-moving industry. Bitcoin has become digital gold, a safe haven in the eyes of some, even while it remains volatile. Major corporations now hold Bitcoin as part of their treasury, and financial institutions, which once mocked it, are now knee-deep in blockchain projects of their own. We even have countries experimenting with Bitcoin as legal tender—a bold and perhaps misguided attempt to leapfrog traditional banking systems. But if there's anything that's clear, it's that the experiment isn't over.

In retrospect, Mt. Gox was a failure. But it was a glorious failure, one that helped pave the way for a larger, messier, and somehow more durable system. Karpelès may not have been the right person to lead Bitcoin into the future, but he was certainly the right person to help launch it into the public consciousness. For better or worse, we needed that implosion, that moment of collapse, to believe in the possibility of what could come next.

The question isn't whether cryptocurrency will change the economy—it already has. The question now is how much more of our lives will become entangled with it, and whether we're ready for the ride. As for me, I can't say I understand it all. But then again, I don't have to. In the end, it seems the secret to surviving in this world of Bitcoin and blockchain isn't understanding—it's just believing. And if there's anything we've learned from 2014 onwards, it's that people are more than willing to do just that.

As I sit here writing this introduction, I'm drinking New Orleans coffee—with chicory—from an aqua-blue large coffee mug, emblazoned with the symbol for Bitcoin in white. Underneath it are the words, "BITCOIN CAFÉ"; that was the name of the café that Karpelès intended to open on the first floor of Mt. Gox. It's all that remains of what was once a billion-dollar business.

It's a damn fine coffee cup, though.

Prologue

Before the police knocked on the door, they called, and a week before they called, they politely leaked to the Japanese press that they would be arresting Mark Karpelès, the former CEO of failed Tokyo-based bitcoin exchange, Mt. Gox. Mark knew he was going to be arrested, I knew he was going to be arrested, my journalist partner Nathalie-Kyoko Stucky knew he was going to be arrested—and she was, in fact, waiting there at this tiny apartment with him and his cat for the police to come so we could have the scoop. We all knew that Mark was going to be arrested and sent to jail, and we all sort of hoped that still, somehow, it wasn't going to happen. Nathalie and I didn't know if he was innocent or guilty, but we did know that in Japan, the working motto of the police is guilty until proven guilty—and in the court of public opinion, Mark had already been tried and convicted.

The Nikkei Newspaper, Japan's most-read business daily had announced the arrest, in the July 31 edition of the newspaper, one day before the actual arrest. The article didn't make a lot of sense, but it covered the basics. If you put all the pre-arrest "scoops" together, they read something like this:

Mt. Gox Scandal Takes a Dramatic Turn: CEO Faces Imminent Arrest for Manipulating Bitcoin Bank Accounts

The notorious collapse of Mt. Gox, the virtual currency exchange that lost an enormous amount of bitcoin, is back in the spotlight! The Metropolitan Police Department is now building a case against the company's embattled CEO on charges of fraudulently producing and using private electromagnetic records, according to an official connected to the investigation. And here's the bombshell—sources indicate that the police may arrest the CEO very soon. He's suspected of manipulating the system to artificially inflate the bitcoin balance of fake accounts—yes, you read that right, fake accounts!

The French CEO of Mt. Gox's operating company, based in Tokyo's Shibuya district, is already in hot water as the company undergoes bankruptcy proceedings. Now, investigators are turning up the heat, eyeing corporate embezzlement charges too. The allegations suggest that deposited funds were misappropriated by fulfilling bitcoin buy orders from nonexistent accounts—sounds like a script for a financial thriller!

Remember last year when the CEO boldly claimed in a press conference that external cyber-attacks were to blame for the disappearance of a staggering 650,000 bitcoins?

Well, it seems the truth could be much murkier. Some of those bitcoins, previously thought to be gone for good, may never have existed at all. At today's exchange rate, that missing haul would be worth around 23 billion yen!

Mt. Gox was once the behemoth of bitcoin, controlling a whopping 70 percent of the global market share. But in February of last year, the company fell from grace, filing for civil rehabilitation at the Tokyo District Court. By April, the court gave the final blow, kicking off bankruptcy proceedings. The rise and fall of Mt. Gox is nothing short of a cautionary tale—one that's still unraveling, with shocking twists at every turn, and an arrest potentially looming on the horizon!

It was the morning of August 1, 2015, a Saturday. The police called Mark at five o'clock that morning, before the papers were delivered to the houses of everyone in Japan, with most editions already emblazoned with a headline that Mark Karpelès was going to be arrested that day. One newspaper had even jumped the gun and published the news of his arrest at 2.00 am, online.

The call was a professional courtesy, since for over a year Karpelès had actually been working with the Tokyo Metropolitan Police High-Tech Crime Squad to try to determine who had hacked into the Mt. Gox servers and stolen 650,000 bitcoins (worth $450 million). Apparently, somewhere along the line, Division 2 of the Tokyo Metropolitan Police Department—which dealt with white-collar crimes—had decided, on their own, that the hacker must be Mark. After all, wasn't that the most logical choice, or the easiest way to solve the case? The police theory seemed to be that once they had Karpelès in jail on any charges, he'd crack under interrogation and admit to having stolen the bitcoins himself. They were theoretically wrong—as it would turn out.

A few days before his arrest, I met with Mark, and Nathalie joined me. I laid it on the line for him.

"Mark," I said, "you've read my book [*Tokyo Vice: An American Reporter on the Police Beat in Japan*], so you know how it works, but let's go over it again. The police will come for you. They will parade you past a crowd of reporters, who will have been told exactly when you are going to be arrested so they are sure to take photographs, or video. You'll be held at least twenty-four hours. Then you will be turned over to the prosecution. The prosecution will have forty-eight hours to decide whether to charge you or not. They'll probably ask for ten days more of detention, claiming you're a risk, since you might leave Japan or destroy evidence. They'll do that again and get ten more days. All in all, round one will be twenty-three days or so. And if you don't confess, they'll rearrest you, and the whole process starts over again."

Mark shook his pudgy head a little, and turned a paler shade of white, yet he still stayed calm. I'd met him a few times since his company had gone under, but I never knew how to read him. He was chubby and pale, and his hair was long and slightly curly. His nose looked like it had been plastered onto his face when it was still clay and then pushed down a bit. He was usually in a T-shirt, and his default facial expression seemed to be a whimsical smirk or quizzical smile. I understood why some employees had compared him to the

Cheshire Cat in *Alice in Wonderland*.

The café, called Café Trois Chambres ("Café Three Rooms" or "Three-Room Café"), was a wonderful old place in Shimokitazawa. It was a cozy, intimate spot, with wooden tables, a lot of charm, sophistication, and a bit of mystery—like wandering through a little Parisian hideaway with just enough space to tuck away your secrets. It was always dark, but tastefully lighted. They didn't serve booze per se, but I ordered an Irish coffee, which contained a solid shot of Irish whisky. A Sonny Rollins album was playing on the stereo.

The coffee, served in tiny porcelain cups on matching saucers, was delicious, and their thick buttery and crispy cinnamon sugar toast was fantastic.

Unfortunately, Mark seemed more focused on the toast than the issues at hand.

I wasn't sure I was getting through to him. There always seemed to be a lag time in our conversations, like the kind you used to get when you'd call someone from overseas on a rotary-dial phone. You may be too young to remember what that was like, but it makes for a strange conversation. You're not quite sure that you're being heard.

"Do you understand what I'm saying?"

I felt like I needed to ask.

He nodded. "I have not done anything. I am not guilty."

He said this with a slight tone of indignation.

"It doesn't matter to them," I told him. "They'll make you guilty. They've already reached that conclusion."

I tapped my index finger on the table where we were sitting.

"Do not confess to anything. Do not sign anything. If you make any statement, make it in French. Japanese prosecutors hate to take on anything less than a slam-dunk case. That's why they have a 99 percent conviction rate—they dump the hard cases.

"Make it hard for them. You sign nothing in Japanese—even though you can read Japanese.

"They will bully you, chum up to you, promise you a lighter sentence if you confess, deny you access to your lawyer, promise you access to your lawyer, lie to you about testimony they don't have and evidence they don't have, and will do everything to break your spirit.

"You shouldn't confess. No matter how many times you're arrested, no matter how many charges they throw at you—you stick it out. Because twenty-three days, forty-six days, or possibly sixty-nine days may feel like forever—but it's a lot less time than three or four years in a Japanese jail. Trust me."

Mark nodded. "I trust you know what you are talking about. I will be ready."

"Dress nicely. Try to look good. Stand with your head tall. Be ready. It may be the last time people see you on their TV screens for a long time. Look professional. Look upstanding. Be ready."

"I understand. Should be fine. I will be ready."

He wasn't.

Mark stayed up all night, not bothering to shave or fully prepare to be carted away at 6.00 am. Nathalie called me just after the police had called to let him know they were on the way. She let me know that reporters had been huddled outside the house for hours.

I told her to make him dress nicely.

Just before the police came, he threw on a blue T-shirt

emblazoned with the English words, "Effortless French", and to cover his face, a black-and-white baseball cap that was modeled after Monokuma, a robot bear character in a popular video game series.

The police read him his rights as they tried to move Nathalie off to the corner. Although he had volunteered to turn himself in on Friday after the *Nikkei* article came out, they cuffed him anyways. The show had to go on.

Meanwhile, I was getting in touch with our editor, Christopher Dickey, the foreign editor at *The Daily Beast*, one of the largest online magazines in the United States. We'd been following the story for over a year. I was sure that the *Beast* would want the scoop—in real time. After all, Dickey was in Paris—so he'd surely understand the importance of a French citizen getting busted by the Japanese police in what was the world's biggest cyber-heist. I had this vision of him waiting breathlessly by his computer for me to send him a news bulletin.*

We'd given them a heads-up the day before—that Karpelès was going to be arrested. The response from Dickey: "Can you write it up for The Cheats section?"

The Cheats section? I was dumbstruck.

It was the equivalent of page three of a newspaper in terms of *Daily Beast* real estate. As far as Dickey was concerned, the fact that Karpelès was going to be arrested, whether innocent or guilty, was a foregone conclusion. He wasn't surprised. I

---

* Christopher Dickey passed away in Paris, France, during the pandemic, on July 16, 2020 at the age of sixty-eight. He was a wonderful editor and journalist, one of the few who doubted the so-called intelligence on Iraq's weapons of mass destruction and opposed the war. He predicted it would be a disaster, and he was right.

guess I shouldn't have been surprised, either.

While I was writing him back and forth, Nathalie was watching the police haul off Karpelès, very politely and almost apologetically.

They allowed him to cover the handcuffs with his shirt as they escorted him through the front door on the first floor past the hordes of waiting mass media.

The T-shirt and the baseball cap did not escape notice.

The Monokuma baseball cap, in particular, was a source of wonder to Japan's *otaku,* anime, manga, and video game fans. In the game series, Monokuma, is given the lines: "Every human has regrets, has things they'd like to go back and change. But I don't! 'Cause I'm a bear." The implications of that simple choice seemed profound at the time, for those versed in the world of video games. To the general public, it just looked like a stupid hat. That wasn't the look I was hoping he'd go for. The cops took off his cap as they pushed him into the back of a police car, with the mass media in close pursuit.

As for the T-shirt, the meaning of Effortless French was open to interpretation. Japan's leading conservative newspaper, *Sankei Shimbun,* which had followed the case closely, translated it as follows: "A French person who doesn't make any effort."

And as I watched the news, shaking my head, it seemed to make sense that Mark was certainly not making an effort to clear his name in the public eye. Maybe he was guilty after all?

CHAPTER ONE

Meet Magical Tux

Mark arrived in Tokyo in the summer of 2009 with his cat, Tibane, who had been named by his grandmother, along with a bunch of hard drives, his computers, a job waiting for him, and a determination not to leave Japan again.

He was thin, pale, and hungry, and had packed enough geeky T-shirts to last a lifetime.

To him, Japan was home.

His other home was in cyberspace at 127.0.0.1—the number a computer uses to call itself. France was just a place where he happened to have lived.

It was his second trip to Japan. He hasn't really left since, and he can't leave *now*.

Mark Karpelès was born in Chenôve, in the Burgundy region of France, to a single mother. He's not sure who his father really is, and his mother won't clarify the matter. His full name is actually Mark Marie Robert Karpelès. The *Marie* was an homage to his grandmother, who is also named

Mark—which sounds confusing to me, but, then again, I don't know a lot about French names. Names are important, though, and during one of his trips to Japan, Mark decided to give himself a Japanese name. This is not completely uncommon in Japan—especially if you have a name that is difficult to announce, or invites nervous giggles or laughter.*

Mark, in Japanese, is a pretty benign name—and also, as a word for "marker" or "sign," has been somewhat integrated into the language. Near Shibuya station, there is even a dining and entertainment complex called "Mark City"; no relation to our Mark.

However, Mark wanted a Japanese name, so he chose one metaphorically close to his own. Mark asserted that in Latin, Robert means "red bear" and Karpelès, "castle in the sun." When Karpelès tried to think of a Japanese name for himself, upon advice from his Japanese friends, he decided he was going to call himself Youjou Kumakichi. Youjou refers to castles and fortresses, and Kumakichi to an anthropomorphic red bear character in a manga who is incredibly sexually perverse and is always getting arrested. Perhaps his Japanese friends were pulling a terrible joke on him when they suggested the name Kumakichi. Or, perhaps Mark came it up all by himself, which would mean he has a very ironic, even prophetic, sense of humor.

He was a bright child and a curious one. When he was still in elementary school, he was given his first computer by his mother, who was also very much interested in computers.

---

* For example, in my undergraduate years at Sophia University, there was one student named Gary. When pronounced in Japanese, Gary sounds exactly like "geri," which means diarrhea, a word that invokes discomfort and invites explosive laughter. We all suggested he come up with a Japanese pseudonym.

She was raising Mark by herself, and she doted on him. The computer was a Sinclair ZX Spectrum, a home computer that was popular in France at the time. (If you are one of those people who can remember when Radio Shack sold the TRS-80, it would seem familiar. It had 128 kilobytes of ram with a tape recorder incorporated—an 8-bit home computer.) With her help, he started to create basic programs on it immediately, things such as drawing pictures of dinosaurs. His mother gave him some computer games, which he would try to modify for fun. He liked to break things apart to understand how they worked; he would dismantle household goods, such as a calculator, to better figure out how they worked.

Of course, the problem with breaking things apart to see how they work is that sometimes you can't put them back together. It's a lesson that never quite computed for Mark.

Mark was fascinated with his computer, and he felt very much at home coding on it. By all accounts, he was an exceptionally bright child, which wasn't always to his benefit. Public school didn't go well because he was so far ahead of the others in his class. His teacher scolded him for counting to one hundred when she was only teaching the students to count to thirty. He was already able to read and write. He found computer programming a language that felt more natural to him than French.

His mother put him in a school for gifted children. "I was not happy with his teachers, who seemed more concerned about keeping everyone at the same level rather than helping Mark achieve his potential," she said. Classes were based on intelligence and ability, rather than age. Some classes would have six-year-old students studying alongside twelve-year-old students.

His mother decided that a Catholic boarding school might be best for him, and he was sent to the Prieuré de Binson, in Marne, for the next five years of his secondary education, from the ages of about eleven to sixteen.

It was in boarding school that he started to check out of this world and into a virtual one. He sought escape from school and the bullies that preyed on him in the world of cyberspace. He found refuge in Japan, or rather the fantasy landscape of Japan that you find in anime, manga, and video.

When he was seventeen—and after failing his year at the Lycée Claude-Bernard high school—he told his mother that he did not wish to go to school anymore. She convinced him that if he spent two years at the vocational school Lycée Louis Armand in Paris, he could get a degree in electrical engineering, and could become the equivalent of an electrician and earn a decent living. He didn't formally study computer engineering like most French software developers usually do.

Mark didn't fit in at Lycée Louis Armand either. He had problems with the school thugs, and was also bullied by people he thought were his friends. Life in a tiny apartment shared with his mother gave him little privacy. He left home, and decided to live wherever he could find a home. He wandered the streets of Paris for weeks distributing flyers for a cybercafé near the neighborhood of Châtelet.

In Paris, where most apartment buildings don't have locks but instead have electronic doors that require a code to get in, Mark would simply watch the codes being punched in and then let himself in at night. He found that in buildings with elevators, almost no one would climb the stairs to the third floor, and he could get a decent night's sleep there. "Wooden stairs were nicer than concrete," he explains. The money he had made during the day allowed him to buy food at night. He spent some of his meager funds on connecting to the net at cybercafés.

During his forays into the internet, days spent in a cybercafé, and long nights spent on his computer, Karpelès became fascinated with Japan—at least the futurist anime version of it he took to be reality. To him, it seemed like a place where he could finally fit in, where a cyber geek would be appreciated—if he ever got there. Mark believed in the possibility of new worlds, worlds like those depicted in *The Ghost in The Shell*, where sentience could exist outside the body and roam free through cyberspace, inhabiting robots, or machines—unrestricted and unfettered by physical limitation. He was becoming fascinated by cosplay, a combination of the words for "costume" and "play"—people dressing up as the characters from their favorite Japanese graphic novels, video games, or animation (anime).

Japan and coding: These were the two things he knew he loved.

One of Mark's few hobbies was playing GraalOnline, a 2D online role-playing game with multiplayer features that was uncannily similar to Nintendo's Legend of Zelda series. At the same time, unrelated to gaming, he created his own cyber identity, "Magical Tux", an homage to the penguin that is the symbolic mascot of the Linux operating system. He was an accomplished programmer by the time he was seventeen, although some would call him a hacker.

Mark had found himself.

In a French documentary, "Suck My Geek", Mark appears

as a member of the new "cyber geek" community. Geek, as you know, originally was a term for carnival performers who did disgusting acts, like biting the head off a live chicken. But just as "yakuza," which is a term that essentially means "loser," became a badge of honor and a term that Japan's mafia used to refer to themselves, the cyber enthusiasts in France embraced the term "geek" to describe themselves.

Xavier Sayanoff, one of the documentary filmmakers who worked on "Suck My Geek," told me that he found Mark quite charming. "We expected someone who would be sullen and uncommunicative. Socially inept—but in fact he was quite charming and vivacious. Although strange. He could walk through the streets typing on his computer, in the rain. When he was in the zone, he was oblivious to the outside world."

He also added, "I didn't think we'd ever do a sort of sequel to that film featuring Mark, but it's funny how things work out. When I look back at that film now, I can see how Mark got to where he is now."

In "Suck My Geek", we see Mark in his messy room, dominated by a computer, a large screen, his keyboard, and some pizza boxes. He's wearing a black T-shirt saying "There's no place like 127.0.0.1."

By this time, he'd already created a name for himself in the bulletin boards and forums of France under his Magical Tux guise. He was a very active member of the online community. It was one of the reasons the producers located him for the film. Mark said, "In real life, if I want to talk with someone in the subway, I am just a nobody. Whereas when I go on the net, I am Magical Tux."

He had a sense of humor about himself, and he knew how to play for the cameras.

One of Mark's friends would later tell me, "The Mark you see on the screen in that documentary is the Mark that he wants you to see, the one the producers wanted to see. It's a reality-based performance, but it's a performance."

If that was the case, it was a very good performance.

Mark's mother makes an appearance as well, and Mark revealed that she was also an internet junkie—playing games online, even creating video game servers—which he found amusing and slightly befuddling.

In the documentary, young Mark says with great seriousness, "I cannot think of my life without a computer. It is impossible right now. In the morning I have to check my emails, make sure servers are fine, and talk with several people before going to work. Then, obviously, at my job I am in front of a computer all day long, and in the evening all the same, I do coding, check out a few things, watch anime to have a rest." The entire world was streamed through his computer first. "I spent a certain amount of time segregated from the outside world in the sense I had my own company that provided me an income; I was working for other companies I didn't know. I could spend days seated on my chair. I probably spent five or six months without going out of the house. All the people I know, I first met them on the internet. After, we met [in person] and talked. It's a little bit like meeting in two different lives." He joked that he had plenty of girlfriends, while pointing at the female figures on his screen, joking, "They're all jpegs."[*]

---

[*] A JPEG is a file-compression format used to squeeze every drop of life out of an image until it resembles a faded postcard found in your grandmother's attic. If someone says their girlfriend is a JPEG, they're admitting that their romantic life revolves around flat, two-dimensional figures who don't complain, talk back, or require actual maintenance—just like their Sailor Moon figurines.

He refers to his computer like a lover. "We've been together three or four years ... we're very happy," he says while laughing.

However, Mark was more sociable than he appears to be in the documentary. He had friends. He cooked. He loved to cook. He prided himself on his cooking, including his ability to make apple pie, and at one point loaded an incredibly detailed how-to video on YouTube.

Mark was many things, but shy was never one of them. He liked attention.

And he knew how to get the attention of others. He decided to turn his prowess in playing GraalOnline into a job. He emailed the owner of the website, Stéphane Portha, and asked him if he needed any programmers for development. The response was immediate and enthusiastic. By October 2003, Linux Cyberjoueurs—the company owned by Portha—formally hired Karpelès, who was now eighteen. Portha was a pioneer of cybersquatting on domain names ending with ".fr"—the domain name ending for France. Cybersquatting was once a very popular money-making scheme in which people registered attractive domain names and then resold them at a higher price to interested parties. GraalOnline was of course also a moneymaker for them. Mark worked as a computer technician in charge of creating programs and dealing with technical administrative tasks for the Linux-based system the company had in place.

For a short time, he was happy. He had a job, and he was being paid to code. "I stayed one and a half years at that company before I quit," he said. "I had one or two little issues with the owner. I left my job because I was tired of being exploited. I also wanted to work in another environment. I wanted to be free to leave my job."

Portha was reluctant to let Mark leave the firm. He had become an essential part of the operation. According to Mark, they had a huge argument when he announced he was quitting. Portha warned him, "If you leave this company, I will make your life a living hell."

Mark, unwittingly or dim-wittingly, helped make that true. As he was leaving his job, he transferred some client data on his employer's servers to servers in France and the US. He took over a domain name and redirected it to his own online address. A domain name in those days could be worth a lot.

After Linux Cyberjoueurs, Mark worked at Fotovista, the operator of Pixmania, just before moving to Israel. In Israel, which was in the middle of a tech boom, Mark decided to open his own business. He only stayed nine months, long enough to see his first business collapse—or, rather, "explode".

The Gaza–Israel conflict proved to be problematic. A terrorist blew up a nearby electric power plant, and his web-hosting business was blocked for twelve hours. Twelve hours of downtime in cyberspace is a very, very long time. His business was shut down. Selling computer services in Israel was a good idea since Israel is an epicenter of technology. But bombings were not something he had planned for. In almost one single day, his business went down in flames, figuratively and somewhat literally. Still, Mark was undeterred. "It is failure after failure that makes you get better. You can't be successful if you do not try."

In 2006, he returned to Paris with only one bag on his shoulder. All his other possessions were lost by the airline. For a few months, he lived with M—an older friend and mentor.

Mark worked on one of his online friends to get a job

at Nexway, a telecommunications firm known at the time as Téléchargement.fr. He started working there as a developer, and rapidly moved up within the company. He left M's apartment and moved to 78 Avenue Félix Faure, in Paris's fifteenth arrondissement.

"The work at Nexway was great, and most of my colleagues were nice. I kept a good relationship with Gilles Ridel, the CEO, even after I left the company. Of all the professional experiences I've had in life, those years with Nexway were the most enriching—on all levels."

In the summer of 2007, Karpelès decided to take a trip to Japan with a dozen friends, in a way his pilgrimage to *otaku* mecca (*otaku* being a word abroad for geeks with a great fondness for Japan, and a word in Japan having layers of meaning).

"Just before the big trip, I invited everyone to my home and stuffed them with my quiches and apple pies, under the pretext that I needed to empty my fridge before the one-month trip." It was one of the happiest times in his life.

The trip was organized by people who mostly went by their online names: Hakkai (a Chinese Japanese name), BombStrike, Ookami (The Wolf), among others. Karpelès isn't sure he can even remember their real names.

"We were divided into two groups, and my group stayed at a guesthouse in Saitama prefecture, near Omiya. During this month in Japan, I traveled a lot. I went to Nara, Kyoto, and Osaka. I visited almost all the temples in the region, several historical spots, and, most of all, I walked a lot. And I took a lot of pictures," he remembers. "Would you like to see them?"

I declined the kind offer. Hey, I've lived in Japan a long, long time.

When Mark returned to France, he continued his work at Nexway. But when his grandmother died in 2009, leaving him only her cat, he left France and moved to Tokyo, this time to work there. He arranged to have himself transferred to Nexway's newly acquired Japanese company, known at the time as Cogen Media, and now called Degica. He arrived in Japan on June 18, 2009, with his cat, Tibane, and moved directly into his new apartment, "Fleur Tsuzuki 102"—his first address in Tokyo.

Mark loved Japan. France "never felt like home" to him.

In particular, he loved the quality of life. He liked the fact that he could buy things in convenience stores twenty-four hours a day (there was a dearth of these in Paris), and the fact that all sectors of society, such as the delivery and transportation systems, were extremely efficient.

"In Japan, you get your health insurance card in twenty minutes at the city hall. In France, it is more complicated. I had to wait two hours to get a health insurance card there."

For Americans like myself, I have to say that two hours for free or even cheap health insurance sounds downright utopian. It's one reason I stay in this island country. And Mark is right: Japan issues your health insurance card with tremendous speed—even if you lose it and need a replacement.

Both France and Japan have public health services which are relatively inexpensive and make basic health care affordable and easily accessible. He was glad Japan had such a system in place.

He also liked the fact that, when he left his laptop on park benches, Japanese people brought it back to him every time. In Paris, he said, people would have simply stolen it.

Of course, a man who leaves his laptop on a park bench, expecting it to come back, may not be the best person to handle cybersecurity for a firm handling hundreds of millions of dollars but that's another story altogether.

Mark admired the Japanese for their politeness. It was their nature, he figured, that allowed him to integrate into their society. People on the subway in Japan are polite even if they are in a bad mood, he noted. In France, it was the total opposite. "Every morning when I took the subway up to [Paris Metro station] Opéra, I clutched my bag in fear of being robbed."

But the thing he liked most about Japan was its anime culture. In Akihabara, a mecca for anime and manga subcultures, he used to spend time in maid cafés, establishments where waitresses dress in maid costumes and call customers "master."

A couple of months after his arrival in Tokyo, Mark quit his job at Nexway's Japanese branch, and then worked on his own. He then created his own company, Tibanne, Ltd., which was registered on October 29, 2010. He named the company after the cat he had inherited from his grandmother after she passed away—the same cat he took with him to Japan.

Tibanne the company (the cat's name only has one "n") provided web hosting and software development. Karpelès took care of the hosting services and development himself. He had changed jobs: now he was working for other firms; he was a cyber *ronin* (a lordless samurai). He would provide services for whoever wanted them, no longer a vassal of Nexway. Mark made Tibanne relatively successful. He had a place to live, a little money, and some luck with women—three-dimensional, living, breathing, real-life women.

He wasn't completely without problems. Portha appeared to have discovered that Mark had diverted data and domain names for himself years before. Mark offered to resell Portha the domain names and data he had diverted for a fee of $2,700. Portha didn't take the offer, and instead filed a criminal complaint.

Because Mark never showed up for court, he was convicted.

In his own blog, Mark admitted that he had been arrested twice in France before he was twenty-one. One charge was related to computer fraud, which resulted in a three-month suspended sentence. Mark dismissed it as a case of hacking gone wrong, without going into details. But if Mark had done crazy things in the past, as we all do, in Japan he appears to have seen the light and gone straight. Tibanne was making him legitimate fiat money—and expanding his horizons.

It was through his company that he encountered bitcoin.

In 2010, William Waisse—a French friend and client of his, based in Peru—asked if he could pay Mark for his services in Bitcoin. Mark had no idea what he was talking about at first but as Waisse explained the system to him, he was fascinated.

Mark was someone who found quantum physics fascinating, who loved coding, problem-solving, and technology, and he found a sublime beauty in the system Satoshi Nakamoto had designed to create Bitcoin.

"It was a beautiful concept. A grand experiment and open source—the cryptologic elements were also complex and seemed foolproof. Of course, I was interested. It fascinated me."

It had occurred to him that with the right platform, he

could create a Bitcoin exchange that would make buying, selling, and using the virtual currency much easier.

When that chance came to him, he was more than ready.

CHAPTER TWO

Searching for Satoshi Nakamoto

During the period that Mark was discovering Bitcoin, I was discovering new worlds as a journalist. For Mark, being introduced to Bitcoin changed his life. It took two disasters—both occurring almost simultaneously—to change my life. By 2010, *Tokyo Vice*, my first book, had been published in several languages, and I continued to write about Japan. I had begun working on *The Last Yakuza*, and was continuing to do pretty much everything I'd always done as a journalist. My focus was still on crime reporting, and the yakuza and the harm they did to Japanese society were my main areas of interest. I was also working as a part-time private eye of sorts, doing due diligence on companies infiltrated by or associated with the yakuza and other anti-social forces.

The yakuza were and still are, to some extent, a fascinating subculture of Japan, but then something happened while I was a guest at the yakuza film festival in New York sponsored by the Japan Society. The title of the event, part of the Globus

Film Series, was *Hardest Men in Town: Yakuza Chronicles of Sin, Sex & Violence,* and I had been invited as a speaker.

I gave a lecture on March 10 at 6.00 pm, titled "Yakuza in Popular Media & Real Life: Cracks & Chasms."

During the event, I got to meet Paul Schrader, the screenwriter of *Taxi Driver*. Schrader had also created a great gangster film, *The Yakuza,* produced by Sidney Pollack and starring Robert Mitchum and Japanese yakuza film icon Ken Takakura, in the 1970s.

After coming home to my hotel late, I called a client in Japan who had asked me to look into a listed Japanese company with organized-crime ties. As I was touching base, he remarked, "The building is shaking."

A few seconds later, I heard bookshelves falling over.

"Jake, this seems like quite an earthquake."

"Get out of the building. We'll talk later," I told him, and he said, "Got it. Will do."

The phone went dead.

It was March 11, 2011, the day of the Great Tohoku Earthquake. On the same day, the nuclear meltdown in Fukushima started— as a direct result of the forty-year-old water pipes in reactor one falling apart. Phone lines went down. My plane back was canceled. I wondered if everyone I knew and loved was okay. The only means of communication that seemed to be working in Japan was Twitter.

It was around this time that Lucas Wittmann at the *Daily Beast* reached out and asked me if I could get him anything on the earthquake, any sort of story. I explained to him that I was in New York, not Japan, but trying to get back.

I did manage to reach a few people. One of them was a yakuza boss I considered a friend of sorts, and he told me that he and other yakuza were loading up trucks of food and supplies to take to the devastated areas. I was skeptical, but he sent videos. I realized there was a good story in that— "Yakuza To The Rescue." It would be the first story I wrote for *The Daily Beast*.

I talked to Lucas, and started writing as I headed back to Japan—heading back to a place where it seemed that nuclear disaster loomed. I feared the worst. I was worried about my friends and my French roommate Camille, still in Tokyo. I bought potassium iodine, toilet paper, ready-to-eat foods, and other supplies to take back to Japan and give to the yakuza to carry to victims of the disaster; they were responding to the crisis faster and more efficiently than the Red Cross. The potassium iodine was to protect the younger yakuza from thyroid cancer, as they were heading into the radiated disaster zones.

I think I might have gone with them for a story if I hadn't got back home to Tokyo to discover that I had my own personal disaster waiting for me.

It was eerie enough being one of the few passengers on the plane returning to an almost empty Narita airport and stopping by an empty 7-Eleven on my way home, where all the toilet paper was gone and the shelves bare, but what was waiting for me in my mailbox was even more of a shock.

The results of my extensive medical check-up before leaving for New York had come back. The doctors had found what appeared to be an over-three-centimeter-sized tumor in my liver. Liver cancer.

It seemed like the world was ending all at once. I had an ominous feeling that everything was going bad. It turned out that my gut instincts weren't so far off. Years later, when interviewing Naoto Kan, who had been prime minister at the time, he told me that he had seriously considered evacuating Tokyo and there had been a serious risk that all the reactors in Fukushima would melt down in succession. It was only the US military and the self-defense forces sharing knowledge and working together that had prevented a great deal of Japan from becoming an atomic wasteland.

On my birthday, March 28, I reconsidered my life and the focus of my work. As I learned more about all the warning signs that had been missed or ignored or covered up before the nuclear meltdown at the Tokyo Electric Power Company's (TEPCO's) power plant in Fukushima, I had a simple realization.

There were far worse things than the yakuza in Japan. TEPCO was one of them. The Liberal Democratic Party, the political party that had empowered TEPCO to get away with ignoring needed safety measures, and had foolishly promoted nuclear energy in a country in the middle of the so-called ring of fire, was one of them. The yakuza were just one social ill, not the root of all evils.

And so I took a break from studying organized crime and began studying the history of nuclear power in Japan, the accidents that had already happened, and why this one had taken place. I began writing about the nuclear meltdown and related problems.

When the Liberal Democratic Party of Japan (LDP) took back power in 2012 and began to bring Abenomics (Shinzo Abe's reworking of trickle-down economics) into play, I watched them turn back the social progress Japan had made. I saw Japan's press freedom decline from eleventh in the world to number seventy-two. The gap between the rich and the poor grew greater. The nuclear reactors restarted. Prime Minister Shinzo Abe started to try to rewrite history.

The Olympus scandal, involving over a billion dollars of accounting fraud, showed what happened when an honest CEO, in this case, a foreigner, Michael Woodford, tried to do the right thing and expose corruption. In modern Japan, it seemed that no good deed went unpunished. The company and Japan's mainstream press tried to destroy the loyal employee who wanted to save the company.

Suddenly, I found myself writing about a lot more than just the yakuza. The social injustices, the changes in society, and the problems Japan faced became my areas of interest.

The Atlantic Wire, where I had been writing for years, was shuttered, and I moved on to writing more for *The Daily Beast*. Swiss journalist Nathalie-Kyoko Stucky (who had formerly worked for Japan's *Jiji Newswire*) and I began working together as a team to cover more ground and a wider variety of stories.

We covered cases of Japanese citizens in international marriages kidnapping their children and taking them back to Japan—in violation of the Hague Convention, which Japan wouldn't sign. We covered the complicated case of a cat-loving hacker who framed three innocent people for making internet threats, just to make fools out of the police. We wrote about the Japanese government's unpopular support for whaling. We followed up the case of a Japanese journalist harassed for exposing a fixer in Japan's nuclear industry. We wrote about the Japanese government's secrecy bills, which had stifled and will continue to stifle the free press. We wrote about people having their palms surgically altered—their life-lines and love-lines—in the hope of changing their fate.

We were a great team, working together for almost three years. And then, one day in February 2014, around the twenty-fourth, I got an email from another reporter in Canada. The subject was "Bitcoin heist in Tokyo?" The text, which made little or no sense to me at first, read:

> Hey Jake—
> Have you heard anything about this:
> http://www.thestar.com/business/2014/02/25/major_online_bitcoin_exchange_mt_gox_vanishes.html
> I'm fuzzy on how all this works—but looks like a Tokyo-based Bitcoin exchange just disappeared online, taking a lot of people's money with them…
> Looks to be Americans or Brits in charge of it.
> Wondering if you've heard anything about it—and if there's any hint of organized crime involved, given Yakuza involvement in financial crime …
> Hope you're doing well.

I had no idea what Bitcoin was. At first glance, I thought maybe they were rare coins of some kind, being sold online. I read the link to the article that had been sent to me. I started researching Bitcoin. I went back as far as I could on Google, and found the original white paper by Satoshi Nakamoto. It sort of made sense to me.

I was intrigued. I had no idea that someone had created a viable digital currency, and was even more surprised that it had apparently been invented by a Japanese man named Satoshi Nakamoto—although no one knew who he was.

I also realized that if Mt. Gox collapsed, that would be a huge story. In fact, the crash of Mt. Gox might signal the end of Bitcoin itself. Even I could figure out that the impact would be huge. There were rumors that half a billion dollars' worth of bitcoin were missing. Some papers were reporting 700,000 missing bitcoins.

I called up Nathalie, and we began trying to follow the story. She located a bitcoin aficionado meet-up in Shibuya, and we crashed the event, asking Mt. Gox customers about their feelings, and talking to experts on cryptocurrency who had come to the meeting.

And, out of sheer dumb luck, one of the people I spoke to was not only working for Mt. Gox, but he knew who I was. We had a mutual friend. And after she vouched for me, he told me everything he knew. He introduced me to another source. Meanwhile, Nathalie hunted down the leaked Mt. Gox document that gave some idea of how bad the situation might really be.

The Daily Beast was becoming interested in the problem as well. We hustled to get the story done, and we were right on target. We reported the number of missing bitcoins more accurately than any other news agency, and we had gained an insight into the poor management of the company. We ran our story just four hours before the firm declared bankruptcy.

On March 6, 2014, the newly revived *Newsweek* published a cover story titled "The Face Behind Bitcoin." They claimed to have tracked down the legendary founder, and confronted him at his modest home in a suburb of Los Angeles.

So I noticed, of course, when *Newsweek* ran that story one month after ours. It was shortly after I read it online that I got an email from John Avlon, the acting editor-in-chief of

The Daily Beast. He wanted me to call him.

Now, usually, when the editor-in-chief asks you to call him, that's not a good thing. So it was with trepidation that I made a phone call to New York. However, Avlon wasn't angry with me. He wanted my help.

"Look, Jake," he said, "as you know, *The Daily Beast* and *Newsweek* used to be together, part of the same company, but we've split up. Now, of course I wish *Newsweek* the best of luck. If they've successfully identified the elusive creator of Bitcoin—great for them. Incredible story. But if they haven't … let's find out. If we can nail the story, that would be awesome."

Phone in hand, I bowed slightly. Force of habit. I replied, "Will do my best."

Avlon asked, "Isn't he Japanese? Nakamoto?"

I replied, saying only what I knew: "John, it seems like he has a Japanese name. It's not a common name, not with those Japanese characters. But whether he's really Japanese or not, nobody knows."

John laughed. "Well, maybe you can find him in the phone book. Good luck!"

And so began my second deep dive into the world of Bitcoin.

Newsweek claimed to have located the digital currency's legendary inventor, Dorian Satoshi Nakamoto, living in a Los Angeles suburb. But the sixty-four-year-old Japanese American denied his involvement, and has continued to do so, saying he was simply misunderstood by the reporter, Leah McGrath Goodman.

She had been contacting people with Nakamoto's name, but all her supposed leads were clearly not leading her to the founder. However, she traced one individual with a name that almost completely matched: Dorian Satoshi Nakamoto, who lived in Los Angeles. He wouldn't answer her calls, so she went to Los Angeles to confront him directly.

He replied, "I am no longer involved in that, and I cannot discuss it."

And that was enough proof for her.

After the story was published, the media swarmed Dorian's home. Immediately, some holes started to appear in Goodman's theory. For one thing, Dorian didn't even have a working internet connection in his home. A cryptocurrency genius without internet access should have seemed fishy.

On March 9, Dorian gave an exclusive interview to the *Yomiuri Shimbun*, Japan's largest newspaper, where I had first started as a reporter years earlier. Nakamoto [Dorian] flatly denied being the creator of Bitcoin, and said, "I had never heard of Bitcoin until a few weeks ago." Dorian explained that when he replied to Goodman's accusation in his driveway, he prefaced his famous comment by saying, "Even if I was hypothetically involved ..." He had thought the reporter was asking him about classified work he had previously done for the US military.

There were many inconsistencies with the theory that Dorian could be Nakamoto, and *Newsweek* chose to ignore them. For instance, the real Nakamoto mined himself a fortune and had an estimated net worth of $500 million to $1 billion at the time. Dorian's house was being foreclosed, and, due to his many medical problems, he was openly in need of money.

The Bitcoin community had, early on, hypothesized that Nakamoto was not Japanese, due to the fact that he never used Japanese. In fact, he wrote well in English and used British spelling. Dorian's strongest language was by far his first: Japanese. In an interview with the *Yomiuri Shimbun*, Japan's largest newspaper and my former employer, Dorian also added what everyone else was thinking: "The designer of Bitcoin would never [logically] use their real name." After all, Nakamoto had labored to anonymize all of his personal information online.

The interview, which was a huge scoop for the *Yomiuri*, took place on March 9 and was published online on March 10 at 2.41 pm, Japanese time.

There has been some question as to the uniqueness of the name "Satoshi Nakamoto" in Japan and in the US, and whether that added credence to the *Newsweek* article's claims.

In the original 2008 paper that launched the virtual currency, there are no kanji representing Nakamoto's name. Kanji is a system within written Japanese (one of three systems) that uses Chinese characters. Because of the limited number of phonemes in Japanese, the language is riddled with homonyms. For example, the following kanji can all be read as "hashi" in Japanese: 箸 (chopsticks), 橋 (bridge), 端 (the tip, or edge), or 波子 (a train station in Shimane prefecture). Most native Japanese people's names are expressed entirely in kanji. It can be challenging to distinguish individuals or subjects without knowing the kanji characters.

The first appearance of the kanji for Satoshi Nakamoto was in 2011, in a translation of the original essay posted on bitcoin.co.jp, which is part of the loosely connected federation of Bitcoin enthusiasts. The kanji characters shown there are 中本 (Nakamoto) 哲史 (Satoshi).

Experts contend that there are possibly 40,000 Nakamotos (中本) in Japan. However, in a database search I undertook of over 150 local newspapers and magazines going back twenty years, there were only fourteen hits, and only two people with the name 中本哲史 still alive. One article was about a thirteen-year-old middle-school student, back in 2003. The other was about a teacher and baseball coach in his forties.

Even though I felt like an idiot, I called every single Satoshi Nakamoto I could find. Most of the people I called had no idea what Bitcoin even was, and, to be honest, I didn't really either. I knew how it worked in the same way I understood how my Subaru worked—which is to say, vaguely.

I contacted all those associated with bitcoin.co.jp to try to figure out why he or someone would choose to use that specific kanji. The translation of the essay was created on October 11, 2011, at 6.03 pm, according to metadata embedded in the file. It was not clear whether Nakamoto had been consulted about the correct kanji use. It was not clear whether the translator had simply selected the kanji on their own. It's not even clear that the translator was not Satoshi.

While I was trying to hunt down Satoshi Nakamoto in Japan, the mystery deepened in cyberspace.

On March 7, the person we assume is the real Nakamoto posted through his long-dormant account at the P2P Foundation ("The Foundation for Peer to Peer Alternatives" on p2pfoundation.net), the site where he first published the Bitcoin software and the essay explaining it, a simple message: "I am not Dorian Nakamoto."

But that doesn't mean that Dorian could not have done it himself, if he was the cyber genius behind Bitcoin.

Prior to this message, Nakamoto had remained silent since February 18, 2009, when he responded in a comment to another P2P member.

I didn't know where to look next for information on the mysterious Nakamoto, but I was beginning to suspect it wasn't in Japan.

Japanese cops have a saying, "Go back to the scene of the crime one hundred times." It's the distant cousin to the cop adage of the English-speaking world, "The criminal always returns to the scene of the crime." Take a close look where the perpetrator was last seen: that's where you'll find clues.

Where is the original essay, if it exists? Why would Satoshi replace it with a later version—if he did at all? There were many questions, and answers were few and far between.

One thing I was certain of was that no one had any idea who Satoshi Nakamoto really was, or if he was even Japanese.

I wanted to share notes with someone, so I asked Ms. Hiroko Tabuchi, who worked on the story at the *New York Times*, to form a loose alliance with me. We'd both reached the same conclusion: anyone could be Satoshi Nakamoto.

In fact, I decided, just to see what would happen, to declare myself as being Satoshi Nakamoto. Maybe the real Satoshi Nakamoto would be outraged, and would contact me. It was a shot in the dark.

On Twitter (now known as X, albeit uncommonly), you have your username, and then you can alter your other name to whatever you wish. My username is @jakeadelstein—not very mysterious. But in the nickname section, I chose to rename myself Satoshi Nakamoto. In English, at first. I encouraged my friends and other Bitcoin fans to change their twitter account names to Satoshi Nakamoto. And then odd things started happening.

By March 7, I had already begun getting requests from foreign journalists asking me, "Is that you Satoshi-san?" My reply: "We are legion. Satoshi Nakamoto is many. :D" Some of us in the Nakamoto clan even composed an ode to the mysterious genius:

Imagine (You're Satoshi Nakamoto)

Imagine no fiat currency
I wonder if you can
Just a world of #bitcoin
A brotherhood of man
Imagine all the people living with no cash

Imagine no double spending
It isn't hard to do
No ATM fees to pay for
And no central bank too,
Imagine libertarians living life in peace, you

You may say I'm a dreamer
But I'm not the only one
Buy yourself some bitcoin
Before it hits a million times 21

By the end of the week, I had convinced a solid number of people, in echoes of the movie *Spartacus*, to declare, "I am Satoshi Nakamoto!" We had twenty people claiming the name Satoshi Nakamoto, until finally Twitter banned anyone else from doing it.

I submitted my findings to *The Daily Beast*, and it was published on March 11, 2014, with the title, "Mysteries Continue to Swirl Around the Identity of Bitcoin's Creator." I wish it was a little snazzier, less meteorological, but I don't get to make the headlines.

Avlon loved the piece because it essentially proved, to him at least, that *Newsweek* was dead wrong. This is how it ended:

> *Rashomon*, anyone? The classic Kurosawa film has become the go-to cliché for anyone who mentions confusing events. But, this time, it actually perfectly sums up this tangled narrative. The film presents several contradictory accounts of the murder of a samurai in a forest thicket. The accounts include those of a released prisoner, a woodcutter, a Buddhist mendicant priest, and even the ghost of the dead man himself, who questions whether there is an objective truth to be found at all. Just so with Satoshi Nakamoto, whose identity seems increasingly lost in a cyber thicket that no one can penetrate.
>
> Only one thing is for certain—Japan has become the epicenter of the still unveiling Bitcoin mystery.

For me, the mystery was just beginning. I needed to go back to the start and find everything I could about the man that nobody knew. And this is what I found:

On August 18, 2008, the domain "www.bitcoin.org" was registered through anonymousspeech.com, a website that never reveals the name of its clients. This may have been the first appearance of the word "bitcoin" ever.

On October 31, 2008, Satoshi Nakamoto published

"Bitcoin: A Peer-To-Peer Electronic Cash System" on the online forum P2P Foundation. The paper was revolutionary. It proposed a formula for creating a monetary system that could operate over the internet, without any bank, without any central node—electronic money. The idea had been floated before, but never the way that Satoshi proposed it. Essentially, he had come up with a system for creating digital gold. It was in theory, a flawless system. It had been designed so that, like gold, there would be scarcity, with the number of Bitcoin being capped at 21 million bitcoins (BTC), making it inflation-proof, and also making it difficult to forge Bitcoin. In addition, every single bitcoin transaction would be logged in a public ledger, to be called the blockchain, thus also ensuring that forgery would be next to impossible.

It was a nine-page proposal. The proposal was fascinating, but, without any software to back it up, it was just an interesting theory.

The P2P posting didn't tell us much about Satoshi, but it did tell us one thing—his birthday was April 5, 1975—meaning he would be thirty-three years old when the paper was published. (He will be a quinquagenarian in 2025 when this book comes out.) The P2P forum required some measure of disclosure to log in, but most of us assumed that he fabricated his name and his birthday as well. It doesn't really matter to the Bitcoin community, which celebrates his birthday the way Christians celebrate the birth of Jesus Christ on December 25.

At this point, I realized that Bitcoin's public history wasn't all that useful to me. What I really needed to know was how it works, and why it was created in the first place.

The best answer I've ever read came from a federal court

case in the United States. This is the testimony of special agent Tigran Gambaryan of the IRS. He's known as the Blockchain Wizard for his ability to decipher the public ledger of Bitcoin and track down criminals who use the currency to launder money or steal bitcoin from hacked accounts:

> Bitcoin is a form of decentralized, convertible virtual currency that exists through the use of an online, decentralized ledger system (the blockchain). The currency is not issued by any government, bank, or company, but rather is generated and controlled through computer software operating via a decentralized network.
>
> To acquire bitcoins, a typical user will purchase them from a Bitcoin seller or "exchanger." It is also possible to "mine" bitcoin by verifying other users' transactions. Bitcoin (BTC) is just one form of digital currency, and there are a significant number of other varieties of digital currency.
>
> Bitcoin exchangers typically accept payments of fiat currency (currency which derives its value from government regulation or law), or other convertible virtual currencies in order to obtain bitcoins. When a user wishes to purchase bitcoins from an exchanger, the user will typically send payment in the form of fiat or other convertible virtual currency to an exchanger, usually via wire or ACH for the corresponding number of bitcoins based on a fluctuating exchange rate.
>
> When a user acquires bitcoins, they are sent to the user's Bitcoin address. This is somewhat analogous to a bank account number, which is comprised of a case-sensitive string of letters and numbers amounting to a total of twenty-six to thirty-five characters. The user can

then conduct transactions with other Bitcoin users, by transferring bitcoins to their Bitcoin addresses, via the internet.

Little to no personally identifiable information about the payer or payee is transmitted in a Bitcoin transaction. Bitcoin transactions occur using a public key and a private key. A public key is used to receive bitcoins and a private key is used to allow withdrawals from a Bitcoin address. Only the Bitcoin address of the receiving party and the sender's private key are needed to complete the transaction, which by themselves rarely reflect any identifying information.

Think of it this way: the Bitcoin public key is like a safety deposit box at a Swiss bank. Anyone who knows the number can go to the bank and put money in the box. The private key is the combination to the safety deposit box; only the person with the combination can access the money.

All Bitcoin transactions are recorded on what is known as the blockchain. This is essentially a distributed public ledger that keeps track of all Bitcoin transactions, incoming and outgoing, and updates approximately six times per hour. The blockchain records every Bitcoin address that has ever received a bitcoin and maintains records of every transaction and the known balances for each Bitcoin address.

Digital currencies, including Bitcoin, have many known legitimate uses. However, much like cash, bitcoins can be used to facilitate illicit transactions and to launder criminal proceeds, given the ease with which they can be used to move money anonymously. As is demonstrated herein, however, in some circumstances bitcoin payments may be traced to accounts at traditional financial institutions using the blockchain.

On January 3, 2009, Satoshi put his money where his mouth was, and the first bitcoin was created, or "mined" as they like to say in the Bitcoin world. This first block of data is known as the genesis block. And in that block, there is a clue to the identity of Satoshi Nakamoto and the philosophy that drove him to create a new currency. Embedded in the block of data, he had quoted a January 3, 2009 article from *The Times* of London, titled: "Chancellor on the brink of second bailout for banks. Billions may be needed as lending squeeze tightens."

The world financial collapse and the Lehman Brothers shock was still reverberating throughout the world. The newspaper headline included in the code wasn't just random. It was a way of declaring the value of Bitcoin—by referencing a huge bailout of the banks by the British government.

A few days after Satoshi mined the first Bitcoin, on January 9, Satoshi released the Bitcoin source code and his Bitcoin software ("the Bitcoin client," as computer geeks would like to say). The software was downloaded by a software engineer and notable advocate of cryptography and digital privacy, Hal Finney, who was fifty-two at the time.

Finney had been a cypherpunk in the 1990s. The cypherpunks, a play on the words "cyberpunks," were activists advocating widespread use of strong cryptography and privacy-enhancing technologies as a route to social and political change. Now, in an era when China uses closed-circuit cameras, massive wiretapping, and facial-recognition software to track every movement and thought of its people, the cypherpunks seem very prescient.

Hal Finney worked with Satoshi to get the software and the system up and running. One of the things about Bitcoin that many people don't understand is that while Satoshi Nakamoto conceived it and created it, he worked with other software developers for years to make Bitcoin run perfectly. It has always been a group effort. In fact, only about 15 percent of the code in Bitcoin nowadays was originally from Nakamoto.

Hal Finney described those early days as follows in a post he made in March 2013:

> When Satoshi announced the first release of the software, I grabbed it right away. I think I was the first person besides Satoshi to run bitcoin. I mined block 70-something. I carried on an email conversation with Satoshi over the next few days, mostly me reporting bugs and him fixing them.
>
> After a few days, bitcoin was running pretty stably, so I left it running. I mined several blocks over the next few days. But I turned it off because it made my computer run hot, and the fan noise bothered me. In retrospect, I wish I had kept it up longer, but on the other hand I was extraordinarily lucky to be there at the beginning.

Of course, many people believed that Hal Finney might actually be Satoshi Nakamoto. But Finney always denied this. In fact, in October of the year that Bitcoin was born, he was diagnosed with Amyotrophic Lateral Sclerosis (ALS), a debilitating disease, and his health began to deteriorate with astonishing rapidity. Bitcoin wasn't the most pressing thing on his mind.

He wrote in his 2013 blog post, at a time when he was already close to being completely paralyzed:

> The next I heard of Bitcoin was late 2010, when I was surprised to find that it was not only still going, bitcoins actually had monetary value. I dusted off my old wallet and was relieved to discover that my bitcoins were still there. As the price climbed up to real money, I transferred the coins into an offline wallet, where hopefully they'll be worth something to my heirs.

When he wrote those words, he only had a few months to live. He seemed to know his time was limited, and he was already thinking of his legacy. He wrote, "My bitcoins are stored in our safe deposit box, and my son and daughter are tech savvy. I think they're safe enough. I'm comfortable with my legacy."

Satoshi Nakamoto, in the early days of Bitcoin, stored an estimated 1 million BTC for himself in various accounts—roughly 5 percent of all bitcoins that will ever be in circulation. Hal Finney died on August 28, 2014, and his body was put in cryogenic suspension. For those who believe that Finney was Nakamoto, it should be noted that since his death, there have been no postings and no emails from the real Nakamoto.

However, in late summer of 2014, as I was still working on the Mt. Gox story, it suddenly seemed like there might be one person who finally had the answer.

On September 8, a hacker who went by the name "Savaged" took over Nakamoto's email account, hosted on GMX.COM, which also now runs MAIL.COM.

The alleged hacker posted on Pastebin (a network bulletin

board) a notice: 'SATOSHI DOX [DOCUMENTS] FOR SALE.'

The hacker promised to publicize the essential details of Satoshi's identity if 25 BTC were sent to a designated bitcoin address. At the time, 25 BTC were worth about $24,000.

Many people thought this was a hoax until a Bitcoin Talk forum administrator posted an announcement on the forum after 9.00 pm on September 8. He confirmed that Satoshi's email account had been taken over.

Within hours of the announcement that Satoshi's emails had been hacked, another message appeared on the P2P Foundation bulletin board:

> Dear Satoshi. Your dox, passwords and IP addresses are being sold on the darknet. Apparently, you didn't configure Tor properly and your IP leaked when you used your email account sometime in 2010. You are not safe. You need to get out of where you are as soon as possible before these people harm you. Thank you for inventing bitcoin.

Like everyone else who had an interest in the elusive Nakamoto, I was glued to my computer waiting to see what would happen next. I made a phone call to Avlon, and told him that this could be big news. Everyone waited for the next page of the story, and then ... GMX deleted the entire mail account.

Nakamoto's identity was not revealed to the world, and the email provider, a company based in Germany, wouldn't clarify what happened.

Did the hacker manage to save all the mails before GMX shut down the account? How much information was really in the account to begin with? Only the hacker knows, and they haven't spoken since September 10, 2014. Another dead end.

Every time there's another theory professing that X is Satoshi Nakamoto, or in some cases when an individual comes forward claiming to be Satoshi, I have followed up. None of them pan out. Here are the usual suspects:

1. John Nash
One of the greatest mathematicians in history and the subject of the Oscar-winning film *A Beautiful Mind*. He is no fan of Keynesian economics, but then again, he couldn't code a game of Pong. He's also dead.

2. Neil King and company
Fast Company reported that on August 15, 2008, three days before bitcoin.org was registered by the real Satoshi Nakamoto, King, Vladimir Oksam, and Charles Bry filed an encryption patent that resembled the structure of Bitcoin. The smoking gun was the phrase "computationally impractical to reverse," also a phrase in Satoshi's white paper. And that's about it. I don't buy it.

3. Shinichi Mochizuki
A reclusive Japanese mathematician, but not a computer programmer. I tracked him down once at a conference, and he just laughed at the suggestion.

4. Wei Dai
A cypherpunk and also an early advocate of digital currency. He's denied it as well, and his writing style isn't anything like Nakamoto's.

5. Nick Szabo

A brilliant programmer, but no one can make a convincing case for him.

6. Craig Wright

A shady Australian businessman and information-technology expert who seems to have manipulated *Gizmodo* and *Wired* into writing an article about him being the creator of Bitcoin at roughly the same time, in December 2015—in what appears to have been a very elaborate hoax. A 2024 lawsuit against Wright ended with a 400-page judgment which stated all the pieces of evidence that Wright had provided were merely forgeries as elaborate as they were sloppy. As the law firm investigating Wright noted in a gleefully schadenfreude-ridden article it posted:

> Hard copy documents had been artificially aged with splashed coffee stains, their staples rusted up in record time.
>
> Notepads had been covered from top to bottom in handwritten notes and backdated to 2007–8: but the notepads themselves were more modern, and would not be created until well after 2010 (facts established through shoe-leather investigation over the course of months).

From the start, Tigran Gambaryan and Mark Karpelès both asserted that Craig's claims were bogus and that he was a buffoon. He might be the only Craig to ever make Craigslist look like a pillar of honesty and transparency. At least on Craigslist, when someone says they're selling you a slightly used bike, you know it's only *probably* a scam.

As recently as 2024, Tigran told me, "I have a good idea of who Satoshi Nakamoto really is and I would never say, but what I will say is that it isn't Craig Wright or the individual HBO identified in their bombastic docudrama, *Money Electric: The Bitcoin Mystery*."

We won't name that individual here either, because he asserts that being labeled Satoshi Nakamoto puts his life at risk, and he's probably right.

Here's *The Sword in The Stone* test for anyone claiming to be Satoshi Nakamoto. They have to spend some of the coins that we know belong to Nakamoto because of their digital serial numbers—those coins buried at the bottom of the blockchain.

Everyone would like to know who the real Satoshi Nakamoto is. Some would like to get their hands on the billions of dollars' worth of bitcoins he owns. The Central Intelligence Agency fears that Nakamoto might be able to disrupt the world economy with his 1 million BTC. "It's highly possible that Satoshi Nakamoto is a state agent, backed by a hostile entity or possibly a libertarian terrorist," one former spook told me over cocktails in one of the last bars in Washington DC where you can still smoke a cigarette. He didn't have anything else to tell me of much value.

A former National Security Agency analyst said he was sure that Bitcoin could be hacked, but after spending weeks looking at the code, realized it would be nearly impossible. "It was made by the most paranoid cyber geek in the world. It had to be somebody at least familiar with the basic tenets of cyberwarfare. Every possible attack has been anticipated and countered in advance."

I don't know who Satoshi Nakamoto is, but when he was

active, he was a prolific writer. And yet you can pore through all his messages, his emails, and his papers, and rarely will you ever get a glimpse of the man behind them. Correspondents with Satoshi would try to glean some sign of humanity from him.

"Merry Christmas, wherever you are (if you celebrate Christmas)," wrote one.

There was no response from Satoshi, except a discussion of the latest quirks in the code.

It's a reasonable assumption to believe he's English or spent a great deal of time in England. His writings are peppered with British spellings. The newspaper he quotes in the genesis block, *The Times of London*, is a British paper. (It's also a paper I've served as a correspondent for. That fact is not relevant, but it does make me feel connected to him.)

Stefan Thomas, a Swiss coder and Bitcoin believer, graphed out the timestamps of more than 500 of Nakamoto's online posts. There was an almost complete absence of posts between midnight and 6.00 am Greenwich Time, which could also indicate that Satoshi lived in England, and that he almost always went to bed before midnight.

A Bitcoin developer, Laszlo Hanyecz, who is famous for making the first real-world purchase with bitcoins (10,000 of them for a pair of pizzas) sent hundreds of emails back and forth with Satoshi. He noticed that the answers would only come near the end of the US working week. It seemed to suggest that Satoshi had a daytime job and only had free time on the weekends.

There is a constant strain of paranoia in his emails—fear of government interference, fear of the code failing, fear of Bitcoin being hacked—that gives some of his correspondence a soft-spoken intensity.

He has been silent now for so long that he has become a kind of mythological figure. However, while no one has seen Satoshi in the flesh, there is now a statue of him on display, made of metal.

In October 2024, the city of Lugano, Switzerland, decided it was high time to pay tribute to the faceless, nameless, and possibly nonexistent creator of Bitcoin. Enter artist Valentina Picozzi, who took eighteen months of study and three months of sculpting to create a statue that, fittingly, disappears as you move around it. Apparently, the vanishing act symbolizes Nakamoto's retreat from the public eye—or maybe just Bitcoin's uncanny ability to disappear from your server when you least expect it.

The statue itself is a faceless figure hunched over a laptop, visible only from the side. It's a clever nod to anonymity, or maybe just a reminder of how most of us look on Zoom calls. And in true Bitcoin fashion, the whole thing feels like a riddle. Is it art? A metaphor? A very elaborate prank?

Unveiled during the Plan ₿ Forum, Lugano's homage to blockchain evangelism, the statue also serves as a monument to the city's commitment to digital innovation. Or, depending on your perspective, it's Lugano saying, "We're all in on Bitcoin," while quietly hoping the statue doesn't vanish along with the next crypto crash. Either way, it's a perfect metaphor for the cryptocurrency world: bold, mysterious, and guaranteed to make you question reality.

Years after I wrote the first article about Satoshi Nakamoto, I asked Mark Karpelès about their exchanges over a cup of coffee laced with whisky in a smoky jazz bar. Mark was eating cinnamon toast. I wanted to know what he thought of Satoshi Nakamoto. After all, there was a time when the Japanese police actually asked Mark if he was Nakamoto.

"You know the Japanese name for Satoshi Nakamoto?" he asked me.

"Of course, I do. Nobody knows if those Japanese characters are really correct."

"Well," he said with a Cheshire Cat–like grin, "I made them up—when I was translating his article for the Bitcoin organization in Japan. I just picked the characters that seemed to best capture the essence of the man in Japanese: 'The center of reality and the wisdom of history'. Rather nice, don't you think?"

I agreed. And then I realized that one of the last clues we thought we had to Satoshi Nakamoto's identity was no longer even a clue.

That is the Zen of Satoshi Nakamoto.

The more you think you know about him, the less you actually know.

CHAPTER THREE

The magical Mt. Gox

You can't have a successful religion without a way of spreading the gospel.

If you look at Bitcoin as a religion (and many people seem to) then Satoshi Nakamoto would be God—an absent and precarious God, but God nevertheless. Roger Ver, who funded many of the Bitcoin startups and popularized the currency, would earn the moniker Bitcoin Jesus (even though he never died and was never subsequently resurrected), and Mark Karpelès would be the saints Paul, Mark, Matthew, Luke, and John. Karpelès did more to spread the gospel of Bitcoin than anyone before him. Under his leadership, the world's first successful Bitcoin exchange, Mt. Gox, achieved popular usage and made it possible for almost anyone in the world to easily buy and trade bitcoin. At its peak, it handled 80 percent of all bitcoin transactions in the world. It was the one exchange to rule them all.

The company became famous under Mark's ownership,

but it was an American software programmer named Jed McCaleb who actually started the site. He had bought the domain "mtgox.com" in 2007. It stood for "Magic: The Gathering Online eXchange." He turned it into an online card-trading site, but then shut it down after only a few months.

You might ask, and you should: What is Magic: The Gathering?

I'm going to explain the game here, because it is one of the many things that connects early fans of Bitcoin.*

Magic must be played by two players by default, but is commonly played by three or more. Within a game, players each assume the role of a powerful wizard, with the aim of defeating the opponent through means of powerful sorceries, enchantments, and artifacts, or by summoning creatures to do battle. The cards portray a variety of fantasy worlds that mix classical fantasy (elves, orcs) and mythological (centaurs, sphinxes) tropes with original creations to create a world unique to the game. It's like Pokémon crossed with the *Lord of The Rings*.

Jed McCaleb, a software developer born in the US, was intrigued by Bitcoin as soon as he heard about it in 2009. He was eager to buy the coins, but found it unreasonably difficult. He turned his long-dormant mtgox.com into a Bitcoin exchange in July 2010 by implementing balances, deposits, and withdrawals, assuming he already had

---

* Roger Ver, an early adopter of Bitcoin, a Bitcoin millionaire who is also known as Bitcoin Jesus, was also involved in competitive Magic: The Gathering when he was a teenager, and toured on an amateur circuit. It's not surprising that he would be charmed by Mt. Gox as a Bitcoin platform when he encountered it later on. He would later become a huge part of keeping the company from collapsing.

order-matching in place from the card exchange. In other words, he added bitcoins as another commodity that could be exchanged online. The new site offered trading between bitcoins and local currencies, and was the first of its kind.

But Mt. Gox soon became more than Jed had bargained for. In fact, it quickly became so popular that it required all of his time—and he wasn't willing to give it. One of the main problems he ran into was that people were buying bitcoins with PayPal. Some unscrupulous users would then dispute the charges, forcing Jed to pay back the money that had been sent via PayPal. Meanwhile, law enforcement was waking up to Bitcoin as a potential threat. The specter of regulation haunted Jed.

He began looking for someone to help him manage the site, and found that MagicalTux Mark had been successfully operating a server business in Tokyo since 2010 and struck up a friendship of sorts with him. Jed turned to Mark for advice on managing the site, and then eventually sold it to him for almost nothing.

There's a Japanese saying *"Tada hodo takai mono wa nai."* It means, "There's nothing more expensive than something you get for free." In this case, it was very apt.

In January 2011, Jed McCaleb formally approached Mark to see if he'd like to buy his business.

Mark was in. He bought Mt. Gox when he was still working at Degica, and soon set about turning it into an exchange for bitcoins. Mark had become interested in Bitcoin when William Waisse, a French friend and client of his based in Peru, asked if he could pay in that currency. Mark had always been interested in cryptography and programming. Since 2010, he had felt that Bitcoin was an amazing innovation and that it could become a worldwide currency if only it had the right platform. In the rudimentary system that had been set up to buy, sell, and exchange Magic: The Game trading cards, he saw great potential.

"I was sure I could work with the system and do transactions in yen," Mark said. "Everything was there for it to work."

The more he studied it, the more impressed he was. As an experiment, he hooked up two computers and sent bitcoins back and forth between them. The transaction went on without a hitch. He was impressed.

"I didn't really think of Bitcoin as a new currency. I'm not a libertarian, as are many in the Bitcoin community. What I did realize was that there were payment systems other than your standard ones that were better than what we had. And Bitcoin was very democratic and easy to use.

"For example, my small company at the time, Tibanne, was spurned if we tried to accept credit card payments or process them. Well, you could use PayPal, but not only were the handling fees expensive, it took two or three weeks for the money to actually get into your account—in Japan.

"With Bitcoin, sure, you couldn't turn it into cash immediately but within a week, you had it in your account and you could cash it out. And handling fees? We didn't even charge them until the start of 2014. It was kind of amazing how fast you could get most transactions done."

It seemed to be working.

"I guess the problem was, how many people would really use it? Or, let's say Amazon suddenly started trading in Bitcoin. Well, a small exchange would be pretty fucked. But I saw great potential."

While Bitcoin Jesus and the true believers in Bitcoin (see

chapter two, "Searching for Satoshi Nakamoto") would tell you that Bitcoin was to currency what the internet was to information, and that Bitcoin would liberate the world, Mark wasn't necessarily on-board with that.

Mark continued, "Every organization has problems. France has gone through many political systems. We had a king. We're in the fifth generation as a republic. All systems have problems. But some unity is better than haphazard rule. Maybe there is waste, but then we just need to make a better government. You need an organization. You need rules. You need safety checks—which is a hard-learned lesson."

Mark saw Mt. Gox as the perfect platform to add order to the chaotic Bitcoin world at the time. Of course, others would later joke, "Take a website made for exchanging playing cards and turn it into a platform to exchange millions worth of virtual currency: gee, what could possibly go wrong?"

Many things went wrong even before Mark bought it.

Nathalie and I obtained documents that included correspondence between Mark Karpelès and the original founder of Mt. Gox, Jed McCaleb, which suggests that Mt. Gox was plagued by problems from its earliest days, before Karpelès had even taken over the company. We were given internal documents including emails by a former consultant to Mt. Gox, and then verified them with Karpelès's lawyer, former employees, and sources in law enforcement. McCaleb first approached Mark about selling him Mt. Gox in January 2011. In an email dated January 18 that year, McCaleb wrote to his acquaintance Karpelès:

Hi Mark~

Please keep all this confidential I don't want to start a

panic and I'm not sure I'll do it yet but I'm thinking I might try to sell mtgox. I just have these other projects I would like to devote more time to. Would you be interested? It could be very little up front and just a payout based on revenue or something. There is also an investment group that wants to fund mtgox. Probably around $158k. So you could most likely take it over with some cash.

Let me know
Thanks,
Jed.

Karpelès agreed to purchase the company from McCaleb, and by February 3, 2011 he had signed an agreement with McCaleb to buy the firm, under some very unusual terms.

The seller (McCaleb) wrote into the contract that "the Seller is uncertain if mt.gox.com is compliant or not with any applicable US code or statute, or law of any country." And it included an article of indemnification: "The Buyer agrees to indemnify Seller against any legal action that is taken against Buyer or Seller with regards to mtgox.com or anything acquired under this agreement."

Mark still thought the conditions were favorable. There was no need for an initial payment—just an agreement to share 50 percent of the profits for six months.

Since Mark had already moved to Tokyo, the new Mt. Gox business was based there. It was owned and operated by the newly established Mt. Gox Co. Ltd., the subsidiary of Tibanne. Tibanne was owned by Mark, but, as per the agreement, Jed would own 12 percent of Mt. Gox. To this day, he retains 12 percent of the company.

Mark should have paid closer attention to the fine print.

The main flaw in the deal was *that the site had poor security and had been hacked*. Perhaps he did not understand how that would affect him. According to some sources, a Bitcoin theft *may even* have occurred on the day Mark acquired mtgox.com. Jed wanted Mark to stay silent about this, and got him to sign a non-disclosure agreement.

Shortly after the handover, Karpelès became aware that Mt. Gox had been hacked several times, and the sum that subsequently went missing was a huge number—a total of 80,000 bitcoins, to be precise.

The following email on April 28, 2011 was probably the beginning of Mark Karpelès' nightmare:

From: Jed McCaleb <jed@mtgox.com>
Date: 2011/04/28 22:33
To: Mark Karpelès <admin@mtgox.com>
I can't tell how big an issue it will be to be short 80k BTC [*80,000 bitcoin] if the price goes to $100 or something. That is quite a bit to owe at that point but mtgox should have made a ton of BTC [Bitcoin] getting to there. There is also still the fact that the BTC balance will probably never fall below 80k. So maybe you don't really need to worry about it.

There are 3 solutions I have thought of:

- Slowly buy more BTC with the USD that Gox Bot has. Hopefully you would fill up the loss before the price got out of hand.

- Buy a big chunk of BTC (really just moving the BTC debt to the USD side) If BTC goes up this is a huge win. Problem is there isn't enough BTC for sale on mtgox. Maybe you could find someone on the forum to do it.

- Get those crystal island people to invest ¥. They have 200+ BTC so they could fill in the gap.

  Maybe you could just mine it.

  Jed

We tried to reach Jed McCaleb for several years from 2016 to 2019 through his email and social media accounts, but he didn't respond to us. Jed did speak with documentary filmmakers for the movie *Catching a Genius Hacker: The Mt. Gox Documentary*, released online in September 2023, in which he defended himself. He stated:

> I think people have a hard time contextualizing what it was like back then. When you think of what Bitcoin is like now, I mean, it was just very unclear that Bitcoin would be a success at all, that anybody would ever care outside this small group of like 2,000 people on this forum. And the whole way I made Mount Gox was just kind of on a lark, almost just because I wanted to learn more about, like, how Bitcoin worked. It wasn't like it was ever intended to be like this massive business or anything like this.

After unloading Mt. Gox onto Mark, Jed would go on to develop a new digital currency, Ripple, in which transactions were verified by consensus among network members. He was one of the wealthiest people in the world, based on the value of his Ripple Holdings. In retrospect, his decision to leave Mt. Gox was a smart one.

Kim Nilsson, a computer security expert at blockchain security firm WizSec, who had been analyzing the case, said, "Assuming the emails are genuine considering the timing, both Mark and Jed were aware of some 80,000 BTC that seem to have already been missing before the large June 2011 hack, and Jed was suggesting possible approaches to recovering from it." The question then remains: Did either of them put these plans into action? For example, by creating a trading bot (a software application that runs automated tasks) to cover the loss. However, that is still an unresolved mystery.

In April 2011, 80,000 bitcoins were worth approximately $62,400.

Maybe Karpelès went along with the suggestion, and figured he could bring the number back up as he went along. But luck was not on his side. As he tried to fill the hole, the price of bitcoins kept rising. By June 2, 2011, the value of the missing BTC had jumped to over $800,000.

A former employee believes that Mark Karpelès has not acted maliciously or for his own profit. "He's a workaholic and a geek, but a good-hearted geek. He just has very limited management skills, a little hubris, and didn't pay attention to accounting. He was only twenty-seven or twenty-eight years old."

He also mentions that Mark was weirdly optimistic and that whenever trouble occurred, he would shrug it off, uttering the famous Mark mantra, "Should be fine."

Obviously, it wasn't always "fine."

There were words of praise for their former boss: "Mark wrote most of the code, he created a fantastic [application interface]. It's a wonderful platform for trading Bitcoin. The problem isn't Bitcoin—the problem was the way Mt. Gox was run. And there were certainly circumstances beyond his control."

Unfortunately for Karpelès, he had signed a non-disclosure

agreement that left him unable to discuss the loss, and he faced the Sisyphean task of recovering the missing bitcoins on his own—a problem that became greater by the day, and sometimes by the hour, as the value of bitcoins skyrocketed.

At the time that Mark took over the company, Mt. Gox had 2,000 to 3,000 users. "I figured the customers would grow gradually and then I'd add more staff, and we'd continue to grow. Maybe in a year we'd grow from 3,000 people to 10,000 people, possibly 20,000 people. That was the image in my head."

But the company's growth spurt was so rapid that it was growing more like a cancer than a healthy organism. On April 20, 2011, Andy Greenberg published an article in *Forbes* entitled "Crypto Currency" that profiled Bitcoin. Suddenly, a niche experiment became mainstream. The world awoke to the allure of Bitcoin. The price soared, and so did the number of users. By the end of May, Mt. Gox had nearly 60,000 users.

With all the new attention and the rising value of Bitcoin came new problems. Mark had to go on a hiring spree; they could barely keep up with processing the payments. But that was just the tip of the iceberg. The immediate problem would become hackers—attracted by the lure of digital gold.

However, in the midst of all of this, there was another, deeper catastrophe brewing. Just as Mark was negotiating to buy Mt. Gox in January 2011, on the twenty-seventh of the same month, Silk Road was launched. It was an underground marketplace on the internet for trading illegal drugs, weapons, and stolen data. Transactions were only conducted in Bitcoin.

They say there's no such thing as bad publicity, but the link to Mt. Gox and the Silk Road would drag Mark and his company into trouble they hadn't foreseen, couldn't have foreseen, and would eventually hasten the collapse of the firm.

Some people in law enforcement suspected that the criminal mastermind behind this new so-called Silk Road was none other than ... Mark Karpelès.

CHAPTER FOUR

Down dark roads of silk and cyberspace

The first Bitcoin purchase may have been for a pizza, but it didn't take long for people to find out that Bitcoin was extremely valuable for purchasing guns, illegal drugs, legal drugs, magic mushrooms, hardcore pornography, and all the other things that you might not want people to know you're buying or selling.

When you combine Bitcoin with the invisible internet, aka "the dark web," the privacy protection of a heavy Tor browser, and an online catalog of illegal goods, you have all the ingredients for what is, in essence, an underground Amazon.com: Silk Road.

It wasn't the 6,000-kilometer-long ancient road of trade and cultural exchange between the East and the West. No, it was the first successful online black market, located smack dab in the middle of the dark web, and a perfect platform for buying and selling illegal goods. It was this highway to hell, or a highway to getting high, that would finally make people realize that Bitcoin wasn't just for pizzas and porn.

Silk Road arrived with the new year on January 1, 2011, when an unknown individual who used the pseudonym "Altoid" started to advertise a hidden service on internet forums such as bitcointalk.org. He described it as an "anonymous Amazon.com." (We did borrow that line earlier. That description was so apt that we just couldn't top it.)

The website hadn't launched yet. Altoid was drumming up support for something that didn't exist in complete form, like a movie preview, as if to say, "Have you heard about the underground website where you can buy anything? Coming Soon!"

And it was Altoid who was none other than the kingpin of Silk Road, the person who created it. It would have been like Satoshi Nakamoto posting on eBay forums or in financial chat rooms, "Hey, have you heard about Bitcoin? It's this amazing new cryptocurrency—untraceable, unforgeable, and it caps at 21,000,000 coins. It's like digital gold, man." It was an amateurish attempt to drum up interest in something that had never been done before. And, ironically, it was those innocent early posts by Altoid—a name taken from the curiously strong breath mint—that would eventually undo the creator of Silk Road.

He was very young and very idealistic at the time. The man behind Altoid was a graduate of physics from the University of Texas in Dallas, twenty-six-year-old Ross Ulbricht.

Ulbricht was a cheerful guy, six foot two, a surfer, and a scientist. He looked like Edward from the *Twilight* series, and perhaps his skin did sparkle against the blue light of the computer screen. By all accounts he was an extremely bright and likable guy. I don't think his parents or his friends ever imagined that, a few years after the fateful January when he began a social and economic experiment, he'd be called "an American kingpin" and accused of running one of the world's largest illegal drug markets—and allegedly paying money to have his enemies executed.

Ulbricht was born to two loving hippie parents on March 27, 1984. It's an easy birthday for me to remember, since mine is a day later but many years earlier. If you believe in astrology, both Ross and I are in the first decan of Aries, the most prototypical creatures of our sign. Headstrong, adventurous, sometimes willing to run over anyone in our path to get what we want; fiercely loyal to friends, and ruthless toward our enemies.

Ulbricht joined the Boy Scouts of America, as his father had done, rising all the way to Eagle Scout—something only 4 percent of the Boy Scouts are able to achieve. To become one, you have to have twenty-one merit badges or more, exhibit the Scout spirit, and demonstrate leadership. Let's take a moment here and look at the Scout Laws. A Scout is:

> TRUSTWORTHY. Tell the truth and keep promises. People can depend on you.
> LOYAL. Show that you care about your family, friends, Scout leaders, school, and country.
> HELPFUL. Volunteer to help others without expecting a reward.
> FRIENDLY. Be a friend to everyone, even people who are very different from you.

COURTEOUS. Be polite to everyone and always use good manners.

KIND. Treat others as you want to be treated. Never harm or kill any living thing without good reason.

OBEDIENT. Follow the rules of your family, school, and pack. Obey the laws of your community and country.

CHEERFUL. Look for the bright side of life. Cheerfully do tasks that come your way. Try to help others be happy.

THRIFTY. Work to pay your own way. Try not to be wasteful. Use time, food, supplies, and natural resources wisely.

BRAVE. Face difficult situations even when you feel afraid. Do what you think is right despite what others might be doing or saying.

CLEAN. Keep your body and mind fit. Help keep your home and community clean.

REVERENT. Be reverent toward God. Be faithful in your religious duties. Respect the beliefs of others.

A Scout candidate must also plan, develop, and lead a service project—an Eagle Project—that demonstrates leadership and a commitment to duty.

You could argue that the Silk Road was Ulbricht's second Eagle Project, although whether that demonstrated the Scout Spirit or not is debatable. However, Ulbricht was surprisingly loyal to the Scout code as he began his enterprise—although he didn't stay that way for long. And libertarians really seem to have issues with that OBEDIENCE part.

While his academic life was richly rewarding, Ulbricht's personal life in college hit a few walls, and he didn't bounce back well. He was deeply in love with his college girlfriend, and after making her an engagement ring himself, inset with precious stone, he asked for her hand in marriage. She basically gave him the finger. She not only rejected his proposal, but blithely informed him that she'd been sleeping around with other men behind his back. That was the end of the relationship.

In his enthusiasm for libertarianism, Ulbricht had become convinced that the government was the greatest problem facing modern civilization and was keeping people from waking up or reaching spiritual enlightenment. He felt that the more laws there were, the worse it was for society. Ulbricht believed that people were basically good. He was all about the free exchange of ideas, and it's not surprising that after graduating he flitted from job to job, searching for freedom and intellectual stimulation. He tried his hand at multiple startups, failing every time.

He found some success running an online secondhand bookstore, Good Wagon Books, with a friend. It was during this period that he came up with the idea of creating a completely free marketplace, a place where anyone could buy anything they wanted—the Silk Road. Of course, the problem at the time was that if you bought anything illegal online, it could easily be traced back to you, no matter what payment method you used.

However, when Ulbricht discovered the existence of Bitcoin—which was thought to be virtually untraceable—he knew there would be a way around this problem. And while he was fleshing out his grand idea of a libertarian marketplace, he stumbled across the dark web.

In his diaries, which were eventually submitted as evidence during his trial, he wrote:

> Still working on Good Wagon Books and Silk Road at the same time. Programming now. It's a patchwork job. Don't know how to host my own site. Didn't know how to use bitcoins with the website.*

In July 2010, he rented a cabin an hour away from Austin, Texas. He was cultivating magic mushrooms there, so that as soon as the website was ready to launch, he would have a product to sell and post: proof of life, so to speak. You can't run a website selling illegal drugs and contraband without a supply to start with, so Ulbricht made his own supply.

It didn't go as smoothly as planned. His cabin sprung a water leak, and when the landlord went to fix it, he discovered Ulbricht's massive magic mushroom crop—weighing almost 100 pounds, according to some accounts. Fortunately for Ulbricht, the landlord warned Ulbricht to clear out before he called the police, which Ulbricht promptly did.

Ulbricht immediately hung up and raced to the cabin in his car, cleaning up the evidence, stuffing garbage bags full of mushrooms, removing the traces of cultivation. Like a scene out of the TV series *Breaking Bad*, Ulbricht sped out of the driveway with his starter supply minutes before the police arrived. It was a close call.

However, Ulbricht had successfully salvaged his supply of psychedelic mushrooms, so he continued to move forward. He began posting about the site on websites and online forums, drumming up interest, and he also began making enquiries about how to use the dark web. In these early

---

* Diary entries and blog posts have been edited for clarity throughout.

stages of setting up operations, Ulbricht was careless. This would come back to haunt him.

On January 27, 2011, Ulbricht, under the name Altoid, successfully launched Silk Road. Later, in his journals, he wrote:

> I got the basics of website written and launched it via the freedom hosting service. I announced it on the bitcointalk forums. Only a few days after launch, several people signed up to use it. And then I got my first message from a user. I was so excited I didn't even know what to do with myself. Little by little, people signed up, and vendors signed up, and then it happened. My first order. I'll never forget it.

Ulbricht then waxed lyrical about the excitement of seeing his operation take off:

> The next couple of months, I sold about 10 pounds of mushrooms through my site. Some orders were as small as a gram, and others were in the quarter pound range. Before long, I completely sold out. Looking back on it, I maybe should have raised my prices more and stretched it out, but at least now I was all digital, no physical risk anymore. Before long, traffic started to build. People were taking notice, smart, interested people. Hackers. For the first several months, I handled all of the transactions by hand ...

Ulbricht became very busy. He barely had time to see his girlfriend, Julia Vie, a photographer he'd met in his college drum club. Julia had a website called Vivian's Muse. (She now has an account on Instagram as well.) She made a living taking erotic photographs of women that they would gift to their husbands. She was deeply in love with Ulbricht, and he was fascinated by her. He complains about it a little in his diary, musing upon those first months:

> Between answering messages, processing transactions, and updating the codebase to fix the constant security holes, I had very little time left in the day, and I had a girlfriend at this time!

It isn't easy running a criminal empire, maintaining an online bookstore, and keeping a girlfriend, all at the same time.

About two months later, a message on BitcoinTalk, a popular forum for Bitcoin believers, announced that Silk Road had been operational for a few weeks with several buyers and sellers. By April 2011, Silk Road hit 1,000 users. The rest of the world still had no idea it existed.

You couldn't find it in a Google search.

You had to know it existed to know how to get there.

You needed the address, and you needed a special browser to access that address and see the website, and you needed bitcoins to buy or sell anything on the website.

The anonymous paradise didn't last long.

Silk Road was transformed from a back road of the dark internet into a superhighway on June 1, 2011, after an investigative piece by reporter Adrian Chen titled "The Underground Website Where You Can Buy Any Drug Imaginable" was published on *Gawker*, a now defunct news and gossip website. In that article, Chen explained how Silk

Road allowed people to buy and sell illegal goods, seemingly as safely as using Amazon.com, but using bitcoins for transactions.

It was true that the number of drugs available—heroin, hash, ecstasy, mushrooms—were astronomical, as was the related paraphernalia. Meth-pipes, syringes, needles, bongs: the website had it all.

The article made it clear that "The Silk Road administrator" (Ulbricht) believed that America's "War on Drugs" had been a complete failure: it had not driven down drug use, it had resulted in hundreds of thousands of people being incarcerated for crimes that hurt no one, and it had created the prison-industrial complex.

When you consider that the United States now has more than 2 million people in prison, often for drug offenses, perhaps he was right.

What the article did not mention was that while the site did allow anyone to buy and sell drugs, Ulbricht had established some ethical rules of conduct, just like the yakuza do in Japan. The yakuza ban their members from stealing, robbery, rape, and anything that violates the noble way. Ulbricht prohibited the selling of anything that was coerced, that created victims, or that used force, such as child porn, stolen goods, or violent services.

Remember the Boy Scout rules?

> KIND. Treat others as you want to be treated. Never harm or kill any living thing without good reason.

Ulbricht had a philosophy behind this operation. He wanted to create an online utilitarian society, following libertarian principles. He wanted to give its users freedom of choice and a chance to achieve happiness on their own terms.

"Our basic rules are to treat others as you would wish to be treated," he would later proclaim on the website.

And thus, there were rules. There were violators, but if Ulbricht found them, they were kicked off. Ulbricht wasn't a sociopath.

Not at the start.

However, there was one more thing in the *Gawker* article that was astronomically important: a clickable link that went directly to the Mt. Gox website. Suddenly, every would-be libertarian, drug user, amateur criminal, conman, smuggler, and dark-web entrepreneur knew where to buy and sell their wares. And, also, where to get hold of the currency of the realm.

With one magazine article, Mt. Gox and the Silk Road had become inextricably linked. You might even say that Mt. Gox was the tollbooth of the Silk Road. And, in many ways, Silk Road also helped raise the value of Bitcoin, which helped Mt. Gox. There is no such thing as bad publicity, so they say. A day after the article appeared, on June 2, 2011, the value of one bitcoin went up to $10. Keep in mind that only two months earlier, one bitcoin had reached parity with the dollar. Its value had increased tenfold in a very short time.

Bitcoin was now serious business.

CHAPTER FIVE

The rise and rise of Mt. Gox

A few days after the Silk Road article was published in *Gawker*, the price of Bitcoin surged—it was as if the Dread Pirate Roberts was lending Mark a helping hand. On June 9, 2011, Bitcoin skyrocketed, peaking at a new high of $31.91 on Mt. Gox.

The Tohoku earthquake on March 11, 2011 and the resulting nuclear meltdown in Fukushima had devastated Japan, but the Kingdom of Mt. Gox was located online, and it was not affected. Everything seemed to be going well. Mark was prospering. He'd met a girl at his office, fallen in love, gotten married, and moved in with her. In May, Mt. Gox moved to a new office space in the sparkly Cerulean Towers in Shibuya.

There were some glitches, nonetheless. On June 5, 2011, Senator Charles E. Schumer (or Chuck Schumer, before his folksy rebrand) declared his intention to have prosecutors shut down Silk Road. He declared Bitcoin to be the currency of criminals. "It's an online form of money laundering used to disguise the source of money, and to disguise who's both selling and buying the drug," said Schumer. The attention this got was a bonus for Mark, but Ross decided to shut down his site and take a break for a bit.

Just around the same time, Mark's website had a problem that made him unable to process any transactions for three days. The glitch caused the price of Bitcoin to fall temporarily but quickly.

Mt. Gox's own disaster started.

On June 18, 2011, Mark was woken at 3.00 am by a phone call. The Frenchman who had originally alerted him to the possibilities of Bitcoin was phoning to tell him that there were problems with Mt. Gox. Quickly, Mark confirmed what the person was saying, and in a matter of seconds he stumbled out of bed and shut down the entire system. There were huge problems with the site.

The mtgox.com website had been subject to numerous attempted security breaches since it had gone online. Hackers would try to create denial-of-service situations—and would sometimes succeed.

A denial-of-service attack is simple enough to understand: it's when someone floods a server with so much traffic that it can't handle any legitimate requests, and effectively shuts down. "Annoying" is one way to put it; "destructive" might be another. Unlike hacking, when someone slips inside secretly to steal information or plant something malicious, a denial-of-service attack is more of a blunt-force tactic. There's no subtlety—just an overwhelming, relentless assault that makes whatever system it targets useless for anyone trying to access it. And while no data is stolen, the disruption alone is enough to bring things to a grinding halt, often for hours at a time, creating the kind of inconvenience that feels almost personal when it happens to you.

The greedier cybercriminals had always wanted to hack the exchange, and with the price of Bitcoin surging, it made the site even more attractive to them.

The security for the website was atrocious, and hackers had learned very well of the flaws of the system and how Mt. Gox worked. Now they were using Mt. Gox's own internal system, not connected to the blockchain, to drive down the price of bitcoins and to generate fake ones. In the space of about an hour, the hackers attempted to sell a large number of bitcoins, which caused the exchange rate to sink from $17 to one cent per bitcoin on Mt. Gox. Fortunately, the huge surge in access was more than Mt. Gox's servers could handle, reducing the traffic flow to a standstill, and Mark's quick moves to shut down trading were effective.

However, panic had already set in. Bulletin boards were flooded with frantic messages: "Sell! Everything Now!";"Holy Shit!"; and "We are all fucked".

Two hours later, Mark posted his first explanation of what had happened and what he knew, and said mtgox.com would be closed for further repairs and open again after the problem had been solved. He also made it clear that the bitcoins created by the hacker and used in trades would not be honored, and that all transactions during the hack would be canceled. This made many in the bitcoin community angry—especially those who had bought bitcoins for a penny a piece.

Mark was overwhelmed and understaffed. He had no idea what to do.

And then he was saved by Bitcoin Jesus, so to speak. A few hours after the hack, Roger Ver sent Mark a short email:

Hey Mark,
If you guys need any physical help, I'm available. I can be at your office within ten minutes.

I'm not sure what I can do to help, but I can help with phones or emails or anything you need for a day or two until you get things calmed down.

Remarkably, Roger—already something of a Bitcoin millionaire—could see the Cerulean Tower from his swanky apartment on the sixteenth floor of a luxury condominium. He was close. Fate seemed to be on Mark's side again.

Roger was born and raised in Silicon Valley in the United States. He had a good life in the Bay Area. He excelled in academic subjects and sports (he was on the wrestling team), and even in fixing cars. The all-American boy, he was always exceptionally bright and a forward thinker. At the age of nineteen, in 1999, Roger founded MemoryDealers.com, which made huge profits buying and selling inventory from crashed dot-com startups. It made big money off the tech-bubble burst as bankrupt companies dumped their hardware and inventory onto the market. (In fact, by 2011, the company was making nearly $10 million a year.)

A year later, in 2000, he attempted to run for a seat in the California State Assembly as a Libertarian Party candidate. It may have been during this time that he caught the attention of the federal government for making flamboyant anti-government statements. In 2002, he was arrested for selling large firecrackers on eBay, under charges of "selling explosives without a license." Even after a plea bargain, Roger still had to serve ten months in federal prison in 2005.

It was in prison that he began to study Japanese, and he moved to live there after getting out of jail. His experiences in prison reinforced his libertarian beliefs and made him angry with the entire system of government in the United States. He believed that people should have the right to do what they wanted with minimal interference or bizarre prosecutions from the government.

In March 2011, Roger was at home when he happened to listen to an episode of the popular libertarian radio program "Free Talk Live" that discussed the Silk Road and Bitcoin—two radical ideas in one radio show. To him, it probably felt like country music singer Johnny Cash discovering the light of the lord in the depths of a cave on the edge of death, and he was almost instantly converted; it was what he would later say was a religious experience. He began rummaging through his laptop even while the show was playing. The idea of Bitcoin fascinated him.

"Bitcoin was a game-changer, no question. For the first time in human history, you didn't need a bank, a government, or anyone's permission to send or receive money—any amount, anywhere in the world. It flipped the whole idea of money on its head, kind of like what the internet did for how we share information. It was liberation, pure and simple," Roger told me in an interview in 2014.

Roger became obsessed with Bitcoin at that moment—so obsessed that he did nothing but read about it for days, to the point that he ended up being hospitalized. It was during those days under sedation that he seemed to have his revelation. Like Paul on the road to Damascus, he was consumed with a vision of something greater than himself.

Wasting no time getting into the Bitcoin community and business, he wired $25,000 to a Mt. Gox bank account in New York and began buying bitcoins. His official biography notes:

> The price was still under one US dollar each, but he [Roger] already knew that it was one of the most important inventions in the history of humankind. His company Memorydealers became the first established business in the world to start accepting Bitcoin for payments. Roger then went on to become the first person in the world to start investing in Bitcoin start-ups. He nearly single-handedly funded the entire first generation of Bitcoin and Blockchain businesses including Bitcoin.com, Blockchain.com, Bitpay.com, Kraken.com, purse.io, and many, many more. Those businesses have gone on to raise hundreds of millions of additional funding and serve tens of millions of customers around the world.

Not only did Roger begin accepting bitcoins at his company, but he put up a gold-and-black billboard on the side of a highway in Silicon Valley with a giant Bitcoin emblem, listing the Memory Dealers website—all of this boldly emblazoned with "We Accept Bitcoin." Memory Dealers became one of the first real marketplaces for buying and selling items with bitcoins.

If Mt. Gox was the Bank of Bitcoin, Memory Dealers was the Bitcoin Shopping Mall. Of course, it wasn't until May

2012 that Roger was "officially" dubbed Bitcoin Jesus, but for Mark on that long, long day of June 18, Roger really did appear to be his savior.

When Roger showed up that day, he was ready to roll. With nearly 80 percent of the world's Bitcoin transactions still going through Mt. Gox, the survival of Bitcoin and Mt. Gox seemed almost intertwined.

By the time Mark got to the office, over 1,000 emails had come in from disgruntled and confused customers—mostly in English. He was drowning in correspondence. Roger showed up with his Japanese fiancée, Ayaka, and one of his employees. They sat down and got to work.

They made an odd combination. Picture them together: the dapper Roger, ripped and buff with a buzz cut, wearing a crisp Polo shirt; and the disheveled Mark, wearing one of his usual T-shirts with a computer programming pun. Roger, who practiced martial arts, moved deftly and quickly, like a cheetah. Mark moved more like a sloth.

Mark was impressed with Roger's energy. Roger was impressed with Mark's stoic ability to handle the crisis in his own way. Although the Cheshire Cat smile of Mark's was always a little disconcerting, as was his habit of slightly clicking his head to one side—as if he had emerged from a swimming pool and was trying to flick water out of his ear.

And no matter how dire the situation seemed, Mark was unmoved. His response to Roger's growing concerns, in his heavily French-accented English, was simply, "Should be fine."

Roger responded to complaint after complaint. In the midst of doing this, he called Jesse Powell from Kraken, a leading San Francisco–based Bitcoin exchange that Roger had helped fund.

Jesse, a former *Magic: The Gathering* player, had met Roger on the game circuit. They had become very close friends over the years, both in love with Bitcoin and the martial arts. They took to the task of working through the spiraling backload of emails that were being sent to info@mtgox.com.

Remarkably, Mark had almost no one to provide aid at his end, except for one employee, a young Canadian with no programming experience who had been hired only several weeks before the crisis erupted. Meanwhile, Mark continued to delve into the problem to try to figure out what had gone wrong. It took them nearly a week to sort it all out, a week in which they practically all lived together in the still barren offices of the company. It was like a camping trip in the middle of an office building. But they couldn't stop working on the problem.

The hack was big news. But it took a while for everyone to figure out what had really happened.

During the June 18 hack, it appeared that Jed's administrative account had been hacked once again, and an unconfirmed amount of about 20,000 bitcoins were "stolen." Trading was halted for a week while the security breach was resolved. That same month, the Mt. Gox user table had been leaked. It contained 6,000 usernames, email addresses, and password hashes. Some users on the leaked Mt. Gox database had used the same username at MyBitcoin, a then-popular bitcoin wallet, and had their passwords hacked. Six hundred of them had the balance of their accounts stolen.

On the day that Mt. Gox was back in business, *Forbes*, which had lit the fires of the Bitcoin boom, declared that Bitcoin might be dead. They wouldn't be the first magazine to prematurely declare Bitcoin DOA (dead on arrival).

Mt. Gox was able to recover from this by publicly apologizing and reimbursing the lost funds. But the company would be unable to make the same promise again. After the crash and the restart, with the aid of Bitcoin Jesus, Mark was busy trying to establish a new, functioning Mt. Gox as quickly as possible, even if that meant he had to work night and day, and during the weekends. As he explained:

> In fact, the ambience at the office with all those people made it very hard to concentrate. So it took about a few weeks for the birth of the completely new Mt. Gox, and the process, which I created to allow the users to recover their control over their account worked pretty well. In fact, to my knowledge, Mt. Gox is the only Bitcoin exchange that successfully recovered from such an event. Later on, around August 2011, a system of 'cold wallets' was put in place with the help of Jed McCaleb, in order to increase security. Around that time, Mt. Gox stopped using Bitcoin Core because it was clearly not adapted, and a new Bitcoin management system specifically designed [for Mt. Gox] came into action.

However, Mt. Gox wasn't the only Bitcoin exchange having problems that summer in 2011. A small Polish Bitcoin exchange accidentally deleted the private keys of a customer, leaving 17,000 bitcoins visible on the blockchain that no one could claim.

In late July, a man known as "Tom Williams" pilfered all the bitcoins of his customers at "MyBitcoin," a bitcoin wallet service, and vanished. People realized that no one knew who he was. The value of bitcoin dropped to $6.00.

Yet people didn't give up. Bitcoin increased in popularity and in exposure.

On September 8, 2011, a seventeen-year-old Singaporean named Zhou Tong launched Bitcoinica, a state-of-the-art trading platform for Bitcoin. It was a high-risk, high-reward venture.

In December, *The Good Wife*, an American TV show, ran an episode called "Bitcoin For Dummies," in which a lawyer defended his client, Satoshi Nakamoto, against the federal government. While a fictional story, it also spurred interest in the currency.

Mt. Gox's customers kept increasing. The US federal authorities kept looking for Dread Pirate Roberts.

The price of Bitcoin on New Year's Day 2012 was a lowly $5.00, but it kept climbing steadily—as did Mark's weight while he spent most of his time running Mt. Gox as a one-man show and eating too many pizzas.

Mt. Gox went on a hiring binge. It needed more workers. One English citizen who was hired at the time remembered his first impression of walking into the office:

> The place was full of activity, fancy desks, and exercise ball-chairs, and people walking in and out with bags—which I later found out were bags of money to make deposits into banks or money taken out of banks. The first time I showed up for my job interview, the glass doors at the entrance weren't working well and there was this schlubby French

guy in a T-shirt working on the door with a screwdriver, a soldering gun, and a toolkit. He had slightly long greasy hair and wasn't very talkative. It was only two weeks after working there that I realized the chubby guy in the T-shirt was actually the CEO, Mark Karpelès.

He recalled all this while shaking his head. "Karpelès had decided to fix the door himself. He just wasn't capable of delegating authority, and that's not always a plus."

In the same year, on September 27, Mark, Roger, and others founded the Bitcoin Foundation, which aimed to "standardize, protect, and promote the use of Bitcoin cryptographic money for the benefit of users worldwide." The creation of the foundation made the cryptocurrency universe seem like it was under control. It was all organized now.

In November, WordPress, the most popular blog-host and provider of blogging software, began accepting bitcoin payments. It was a symbolic victory. Bitcoin was going legit quickly.

Sure, there were some problems. Bitcoinica got hacked, once, twice, and went under. Bitcoin exchange Bitfloor went out of business after a hacker broke into the online wallet (hot wallet) and stole 24,000 bitcoins.

This didn't hurt Mt. Gox. The reasoning seemed to be that you took a big risk with small Bitcoin exchanges. If you wanted to be safe, you put your money and your bitcoin with Mt. Gox.

Compared to a year before, the price of Bitcoin had almost tripled to $13.30 on January 1, 2013.

It seemed like it would be an auspicious year for Mark. He had become an important person, a mysterious mastermind and key player in the Bitcoin universe. Everyone wanted to talk to him. However, neither he nor Mt. Gox's customers had any idea of the trouble that was to come.

CHAPTER SIX

Crime pays ... if you're getting paid in bitcoins

Once upon a time, the old saying "Crime never pays" may have been true—but that was before Bitcoin. You might have thought that Bitcoin becoming associated with an underground black market such as the Silk Road would have been a terrible thing for Bitcoin and the Bitcoin community, but in fact it proved to have the exact opposite effect. The price of bitcoins surged.

The existence of the Silk Road made people realize that bitcoins had value. The combination of Bitcoin and an illegal drug market also fell right in line with libertarian philosophy, which believes in as little government regulation as possible.

Whether you're basking in fame or weathering infamy, the spotlight has its perks—any press, good or bad, keeps the wheels of business turning and your name on everyone's lips. In the end, the *Gawker* article was the greatest thing to happen to Bitcoin in years. Suddenly, everyone was talking about Bitcoin.

A few days after the publication of the Gawker article, Democratic senators Chuck Schumer and Joe Manchin sent a letter to the US Drug Enforcement Administration (DEA), in which they expressed great concern and asked the authorities to take immediate action to shut down the site. According to Ulbricht's supporters and family, that's roughly around the time that he relinquished control of the website to his successors.

We're going to stop here and explain a little bit about how the Silk Road worked; and why, despite the outcry, it wasn't easy to kill. The internet is more complex than the average user knows; not everything on the internet shows up in a Google search.

If we were to draw a diagram, we'd start like this: One big circle—the internet. Within the big circle, a smaller circle (but still about 80 percent of the big circle) is the deep web—a general term to refer to websites that can't be explored via search engines like Google or Yahoo. Then there is the final circle within that deep web, "the dark web," referring to any computer network that uses proprietary protocols or that requires special software to access. There are several such networks, Tor and Freenet being the most popular.

The Tor network became the home of the Silk Road.

The only thing you need to do to find it, which any teenager could also do, is to download the Tor browser on your computer, and search places such the "Hidden Wiki," a secret deep-web page that references all the anonymous websites. There's nothing illegal about the browser itself. By using the Tor network, which is part of the deep web, and the Tor browser, you can access sites such as "Rent-A-Hacker," "Create-encrypted self-destructive notes," "Drug Market,"

"US Fake ID Store," "Hitman Network," "Counterfeit USD," "OnionWallet—Anonymous Bitcoin Wallet and Bitcoin Laundry," or "Anonymous, safe, secure, crowdfunded assassinations." Child pornography and other vile materials can also be found if you are so inclined.

Oddly enough, the Tor network was initially developed by the United States Naval Research Laboratory in the 1990s for spying, and is still financed by the US government. It is wonderful at protecting user privacy by bouncing information all over the globe to make identifying the access point to the website, or the Internet Protocol (IP) address of your computer, very difficult. Normally, the IP address reveals what city, state, or country you are accessing the internet from on a map. This isn't good if you want to remain in the dark.

There are, of course, benevolent uses for Tor sites. For example, a whistleblower or a political activist in North Korea (or the United States, for that matter) could use a Tor site to upload and share secret data, or communicate to the outside world, without fear of reprisal. The deep web is full of websites for users concerned about privacy and who treasure their anonymity online.

The Silk Road was a website on the Tor network, and very hard to access without using the Tor browser. The URL for the Silk Road was difficult to memorize, and it was made that way on purpose. If you were looking for "Silkroad.org" you wouldn't find it. Here is the address of the Silk Road when it launched:

http://tydgccykixpub6uz.onion

(That's not a user-friendly address.)

While the Silk Road was and still is a marketplace for prescription and nonprescription drugs, weapons, and other illicit items, there is a strange honesty to the whole enterprise. Silk Road vendors are and were unlikely to scam you because the site runs on a reputation-based trading system. "Our community is amazing," Silk Road's anonymous administrator told *Gawker* in an email. "They are generally bright, honest, and fair people, very understanding, and willing to cooperate with each other."

This is how Ulbricht intended it to be. In other words, Ulbricht expected the Silk Road users, buyers, and sellers to behave like Boy Scouts. Silk Road members were expected to be trustworthy, loyal, helpful, friendly, courteous, and kind: Scout's honor.

They say there's no honor among thieves, but with Silk Road vendors there's a healthy respect for reputation that borders on honor. In fact, one of the special agents who would later help bring down the whole enterprise told the courts he was surprised by how reliable the vendors turned out to be. They tested all the samples they had acquired in undercover buys, and in only 2 percent of cases did the drugs not turn out to be as advertised. Vendors felt comfortable selling illegal goods on Silk Road because the police couldn't easily track them.

Of course, some things, such as fake passports, are probably harder to rate or verify, since if you fail at using them, you may not have access to a computer to write a scathing review for a few years—because you'd probably end up in prison.

Even before the article and the outcry from the US Senate, there was already a team of special agents on Ulbricht's trail.

Jared Der-Yeghiayan was a Department of Homeland Security special agent working at Chicago's O'Hare International Airport. Der-Yeghiayan was a tall, lanky, and stubborn special agent. He had a deep, melodious voice and a certain charm—a charm that made people want to talk to him.

Since the beginning of 2001, he had noticed a gradual increase in drug shipments passing through the airport (at least the ones they were catching) less than six months after the Silk Road was launched. However, the amounts of shipped drugs they seized were relatively small: one or two pills, or a few grams of cocaine. He wanted to pursue the case, but his immediate supervisor told him to give up. "It's a waste of time … We want big seizures." Der-Yeghiayan persisted.

Eventually, he took a chance, and did what federal agents call "a knock and talk." He knocked on the door of one individual who was supposed to be receiving a few tabs of ecstasy. The recipient wasn't home, but his talkative roommate was, and when Der-Yeghiayan pressed him as to where the drugs came from, the roommate answered without hesitation.

"The dude bought it from some website called Silk Road. You can buy any fucking drug you want—and quality shit. You just need bitcoin."

He showed Der-Yeghiayan the website, and the special agent was especially happy.

He was onto something big, he could tell. He started looking at the shipments his department was seizing, and they matched up with the photos, descriptions, and "shipped from" locations of the drugs advertised on Silk Road's website.

He gathered enough shipments to fill a large bin with drugs, took them to his boss, plopped them on his desk, and made his case for making a case. This time, his supervisor said yes.

He was also quite fascinated by the seemingly tight connection between Mt. Gox and the Silk Road. The two entities seemed to be part of the same drug ring. In the end, it would take two and a half years of hard work and collaboration between him, special agents of the Drug Enforcement Agency, the Federal Bureau of Investigation, the Department of Homeland Security, the Internal Revenue Service, the Secret Service, and other agencies to discover the secret behind Silk Road. Their mission was named "Operation: Marco Polo," after the famous explorer of the original Silk Road. It was a better name than most federal investigations were given. (For example, "Operation Tropical Storm" was the nom de plume given to an FBI sting operation designed to capture a drug-dealing yakuza boss on Hawaiian soil in the 1990s. The name wasn't particularly clever or witty.)

While the investigation continued, Silk Road continued to grow. On June 18, 2011, the official Silk Road forum appeared on Tor to discuss the website, and Ulbricht allegedly posted the first comment on the forum under the pseudonymous name "Silk Road."

Seven months later, on February 5, 2012, the moderator who had previously been writing under the name "Silk Road" announced, on Silk Road forums, that he intended to change his name:

> I need an identity separate from the site and the enterprise of which I am now only a part of. I need a name. Drum roll please … my new name is: Dread Pirate Roberts.

The name was lifted from *The Princess Bride*, the popular book and film by William Goldman. In it, the Dread Pirate Roberts is the central figure—a swashbuckling hero, libertarian in spirit. And so, the identity of DPR—Dread Pirate Roberts—was born, and the police wasted no time in hunting down this new character.

The first question they had was whether DPR was one person or several. Later on, Ulbricht would claim he'd handed the reins to an administrator and moved on. But something curious happened when Ulbricht, or whoever succeeded him, adopted this new persona. It was as if the shift from administrator to pirate, the shedding of one identity for a new, flamboyant alias, freed him from the old restraints. Morality, routine, the pretense of having a normal life—all of it seemed to fall away. He was on his way to becoming a real outlaw.

There are times when life imitates art. Ulbricht happened to be a huge fan of *Breaking Bad*. You know the story: Walter White, a mild-mannered high school chemistry teacher, turns to cooking meth after he's diagnosed with terminal cancer. At first, he's doing it for his family, to leave something behind. But as his operation expands, he adopts the name Heisenberg to hide his identity, and in doing so he becomes something else entirely—a ruthless drug lord, willing to kill off rivals and even friends who threaten his empire.

DPR began to loosen the rules on what was allowed on the site. Traffic had grown too much for one man to manage, so he brought in trusted moderators and administrators to maintain the site's integrity.

One of those was Curtis Green, who went by the name "Chronic Pain." A kind, rotund Mormon grandfather from Spanish Fork, Utah, Green worked his way up to become

DPR's right-hand man. The nickname wasn't just for show—he suffered from health problems that left him in constant pain. Silk Road offered him the medication he needed, at a price he could afford. Green handled customer support, helping users navigate the site, and focused on harm reduction, making sure buyers weren't overdosing or receiving bad product. For his trouble, DPR paid him handsomely.

By mid-2012, the Baltimore task force that had been set up to dismantle the network was making headway. But there was more happening beneath the surface. At least two members of the Baltimore task force had plans of their own.

Carl Mark Force IV, a DEA agent, had been assigned to Task Force Marco Polo, where he was mostly given administrative work. It wasn't exactly his idea of a good time. Force had once earned a reputation as an undercover operative, going so deep that his bosses started worrying he was no longer a cop pretending to be a drug dealer, but had turned into a drug dealer pretending to be a cop. They pulled him off that assignment and stuck him behind a desk. When Marco Polo came along, he jumped at the chance to be involved.

Carl was one of those men who seemed to have lived several lifetimes, and somehow all of them left their mark on his face. He had that kind of rugged, weathered look that made you think of Marlboro commercials—if, of course, the cowboys in those ads had spent a few too many years indoors, under fluorescent lighting, filling out paperwork. His hair, when he had it, was the color of a once-bold dream, now a washed-out sort of gray, slicked back in a way that suggested he had either tried very hard to keep it or had given up entirely.

There was a certain heaviness about him, like a man who had eaten one too many regrettable steaks at the kind of steakhouses where nobody judges your drink choice if it's before noon. His eyes, a nondescript hazel, seemed as if they'd seen too much—and not enough of the good stuff. There was a restlessness in them, the kind that comes from peering into too many dark corners, looking for excitement in the wrong places.

He had a jawline that might once have been chiseled, but had softened in a way that comes from too many hours sitting at a desk without moving. On him, it was more like an afterthought, framed by a neatly trimmed beard that seemed to be trying desperately to restore some of the authority his posture had long abandoned. People said his suits never quite fit, hanging on him like an obligation he had grudgingly accepted, the way one might wear a distant relative's hand-me-downs: functional, but never quite right.

Altogether, Force had the look of a man whose best disguise was himself. A face that could blend in anywhere, and yet left you with an uneasy feeling, like maybe you'd seen it before, probably somewhere you'd rather not remember.

Fortunately for Force, he and DPR weren't exactly having video conferences.

Without official clearance, Force began cozying up to DPR, posing as a one-eyed Dominican drug smuggler by the name of Nob. The two hit it off in what could only be described as a bromance. Nob gave DPR advice on evading capture, and tips on concealing his identity—driving his superiors at the DEA nuts with his antics.

By the end of 2012, Shaun Bridges, a federal investigator with the Secret Service, also part of the Marco Polo team, made his move. He managed to connect with Curtis Green, the Silk Road moderator.

And this is where things started to get crazy.

In January 2013, Bridges and Force, along with the rest of the task force, set up a sting operation. They sent a box of cocaine to Green, dropping it on his doorstep. When Green took the box inside, a SWAT team in bulletproof vests and carrying machine guns, accompanied by DEA agents, kicked down his door and arrested him on charges of receiving drugs. He was given a choice—cooperate and turn into a government witness, or do serious jail time. Green was put in jail for cocaine possession, and was then granted bail.

"For his own protection," Bridges and Force then sequestered Green in a hotel room and interrogated him for twelve hours. Both agents were part of the task force, so this wasn't completely out of line. They pressured Green to tell them everything he knew—passwords, transactions, how to log into his account. At some point during the debriefing, Bridges left the hotel. On the same day, 20,000 bitcoins, worth nearly $350,000 at the time, *mysteriously* vanished from the accounts of sellers on Silk Road.

Green also went off the grid.

It didn't take long for DPR to figure out that something had gone terribly wrong. A Google search revealed that Green had been arrested. As far as DPR knew, Green had ripped him off of nearly $350,000 worth of bitcoins, and might even be talking to the cops. He was furious and worried. What should he do?

He consulted the few people he trusted. One of them was Nob—who, of course, was Special Agent Force who now had Green in custody, all unbeknownst to DPR. Believing him to be a drug smuggler and thug, DPR asked Nob if he knew someone who could take care of Green, teach him a lesson, and make him return the money. DPR requested the following: "I'd like him beat up. Then force him to send the bitcoins he stole back ... Like sit him down at his computer and make him do it." He then told Nob that getting the money back "would be amazing."

Nob offered to get it done, for a price.

Agent Force then convinced Green that being fake-tortured was for his own good. He got Green to sign a waiver to allow the agents to set up a satisfactory scene "teaching him a lesson"—like something out of *Breaking Bad*.

Another Secret Service agent posing as a gangster helped Agent Force submerge Green in the bathtub of the motel room, pushing his head into the water four times in simulated torture. Green thrashed around, waving his hands in the air, and screaming. The agent took his job a little too seriously, and Green actually did feel like he might drown. At one point, they yanked Green out of the water by his hair while Force snapped a picture. They sent the photo as evidence to DPR, but while they had been torturing Green, DPR had already had a change of heart—a change for the worse.

He had consulted another trusted administrator known as "Variety Jones," who had given DPR some tough love. Jones had advised DPR that letting Green live would show weakness. Variety Jones, unlike Nob, was a real drug dealer, one who had done hard time. No one would fear the Dread Pirate Roberts if you could steal $350,000 from him and live, right?

Variety Jones asked a rhetorical question that DPR had to struggle with. "At what point in time do we decide we've had enough of someone's shit, and terminate them?" And now DPR, not sure what to do, crossed the line from libertarian idealist to cold-blooded sociopath.

It was also the point in time where he violated the most important of the Scout rules. A Scout is *KIND. Treat others as you want to be treated. Never harm or kill any living thing without good reason.* I don't think William D. Boyce, the founder of the Boy Scouts of America, would have agreed that getting ripped off was a "good reason" to kill someone, but I'm just guessing.

DPR wanted Nob to put Chronic Pain out of his misery.

"I have no problem wasting this guy," DPR allegedly wrote. This was a headache for Agent Force. He'd faked torturing Green, but now he had to fake killing him. Using some bad lighting, and a can of Campbell's Chicken & Stars soup in place of vomit, they shot a picture of the "dead" Curtis Green, making it appear as if he'd died of asphyxiation. Then they sent a new picture.

DPR paid Force the equivalent of $80,000 in the end for the "hit."

I'd like to imagine this was a low point for DPR. Even though no one had actually died, he didn't know that; the belief that he had killed someone must have made him feel irredeemable. Because when he began, before he became "DPR", Ross Ulbricht, like the fictional Walter White, was a man with good intentions. DPR now abandoned his attempts to keep the website up to Boy Scout code. People were now selling assault weapons, hacking software, and cyanide and other poisons on Silk Road. There were no checks and balances anymore. It was as though this superhighway of contraband had all at once had the speed limits removed, and the highway patrol all fired, and thus Silk Road became *Mad Max: Fury Road*.

There is other evidence to suggest that Ulbricht ordered more murders after the first—via the Hell's Angels—none of which were real, but appeared to have been a scam. This is probably why he was never charged with attempted murder at his eventual trial.

It didn't really matter. Once Ulbricht as DPR had crossed the line, he couldn't go back. He began paying more money to Nob, who claimed to have information on the continuing investigation into a corrupt cop.

And Agent Force as Nob wasn't exactly lying either—except that the corrupt cop in question was himself.

Silk Road remained a modestly successful venture. By March 2013, the secret site listed 10,000 items for sale, 7,000 of which were drugs. Silk Road generated $213.9 million in sales and $13.2 million in commissions before police shut it down. However, the total sales didn't even approach half the amount of money that would be lost or hacked from Mt. Gox. Crime does not pay that well.

The FBI shut the original Silk Road down in May 2013. It couldn't truly destroy the marketplace, though. Later, Silk Road was revamped with a revised version called Silk Road 3, which was then shut down again. There are now websites that will tell you how to access the new and allegedly even more secure Silk Road successors, such as Kraken Market, which appeared in 2023. Google them at your own risk.

The FBI doesn't like to talk about their inability to close down the site for good. And the US government wasn't able to capture DPR so easily, either. But they had been preparing.

First of all, Special Agent Jared Der-Yeghiayan had to

infiltrate Silk Road under the pseudonym "Cirrus." Cirrus worked as a moderator responsible for assisting clients and moderating inappropriate comments on the site's forums.

Der-Yeghiayan spent thousands of hours on community forums and organized fifty undercover purchases of drugs while making the case. However, no one really knew who Dread Pirate Roberts was—and then they had a lucky break.

In 2013, Gary Alford, a special agent with the IRS, was assigned to the Silk Road task force. He recruited low-level administrators on the Silk Road, helping to build the investigation but he never gave up hunting for Dread Pirate Roberts.

He had a nondescript ace up his sleeve: Google. He used the advanced search option to look for materials relating to Silk Road in its earliest days. That eventually took him to a chatroom post made just before Silk Road had gone online, in early 2011, by Altoid. "Has anyone seen Silk Road yet? It's kind of like an anonymous Amazon.com."

It was the earliest mention of Silk Road he could find.

On the first weekend of June 2013, Alford followed Altoid all over the internet, sifting through the detritus of cyberspace to find any communications involving his prey. Alford found a deleted message from Altoid that remained online in the response of another user. In that post, Altoid asked for some programming help related to Tor, and in it he revealed his email address: rossulbricht@gmail.com.

How's that for a clue? The Professor Moriarty of Silk Road had proven to be more like an Elvis impersonator in Vegas trying to get a free meal. He wasn't such a great criminal mastermind after all. When Alford googled Ross Ulbricht, he found someone who matched what they knew of DPR to a surprising degree.

The task force was able to locate Ulbricht in San Francisco. However, they faced a daunting task in nabbing him. They would have to catch Ulbricht in the act, with his computer open, logged in as DPR, to make any charges stick.

They knew that DPR had booby-trapped his computer so that whenever he closed it, all data was encrypted and the computer locked down. They also knew that he had created a self-destruct button that would erase everything on his laptop with one push.

They'd have to stake him out and grab him at the opportune time.

During the trial of Ross Ulbricht, Der-Yeghiayan explained that the idea was to get Ulbricht in a public space and initiate a chat with DPR, and then get his computer in an open, non-encrypted state in order to verify that it contained the same chat he was having with DPR.

In other words, if Ross managed to simply close his laptop before the FBI took it from him at the time of his arrest, it would be almost impossible to prove that he and DPR were the same person.

Ross Ulbricht was arrested on October 1, 2013, at 3.15 pm. He was sitting in the science fiction section of the Glen Park Library in San Francisco, taking advantage of the public internet.

Special Agent Der-Yeghiayan was sitting right opposite the library, at a fancy coffee shop. At 3.08 pm, when Dread Pirate Roberts connected to the encrypted chat on Silk Road, Der-Yeghiayan asked him to verify a message on one of the forums in order to confirm if Ulbricht was indeed connected to the site. "OK, which post?" DPR answered back. While a couple in front of him feigned a nearly violent brawl and

Ulbricht turned to look, the special agent inside gave the green light for the arrest.

Ulbricht was wearing the kind of outfit you'd expect from someone who'd spent more time hunched over a laptop than standing in front of a mirror. A red hoodie, faded and soft-looking, like it had seen one too many laundromats and had long since given up trying to impress. His jeans were standard issue—blue, with a certain stiffness that suggested they were bought without much thought, and were worn with even less. He had sneakers on, the kind that made him look more like a college kid late for his sociology class than the alleged mastermind behind a global online drug empire.

While he was distracted, an Asian woman suddenly yelled at him, "I am tired of you!!!!" and she forcefully snatched the computer from his hands.

The woman was an undercover FBI agent, wearing a yellow raincoat. She had told the librarians that the FBI was planning to make an arrest. There were between six to eight agents already in the library. They forced the young man onto the floor and put him in handcuffs. Ulbricht followed them without resistance and without emotion.

And the look on his face—oh, that was something, agents on the case remember. A mix of bewilderment and betrayal, like he'd just been told that Santa Claus was a fraud—and little naughty Ross was also going to have all his Christmas presents confiscated. His eyes widened, but not with the bugged-out panic you'd expect. No, there was something else there, a sadness almost, like he'd been caught out of bounds in a game whose rules he thought he'd finally figured out. It wasn't horror or anger; it was resignation. As if, in that instant, he knew that all the carefully built walls around his life had crumbled, and here he was, at the mercy of a bunch of no-coiners, a mob of clueless normies who were never going to understand why he'd done any of it.

In the car, as he was being escorted to prison, Ulbricht sat in the backseat with Chris Tarbell, one of the FBI special agents who had been pursuing him for months. Tarbell and Ulbricht had a courteous conversation—Tarbell knew so much about Ulbricht that they almost seemed like friends. Of course, part of the conversation was to let Ulbricht know that the FBI knew all about him. Ulbricht seemed slightly amused by the whole thing, but also anxiously talkative.

At one point, when the conversation lulled, Ulbricht said, "I don't suppose $20 million can get me out of this [mess]?"

"No," said Tarbell, gently kidding him. He told Ulbricht that he'd have to pay off the FBI agent who was driving the car as well.

Ulbricht eventually faced trial for narcotics trafficking, computer hacking, and five other charges. Attempted murder was not among them.

The trial lasted four short weeks. Ulbricht's defense attorneys tried to argue that Ulbricht was the fall guy—not the real DPR. They argued that, in fact, Mark was the real Dread Pirate Roberts. They questioned Agent Der-Yeghiayan about his beliefs that Mark must have been the mastermind. Yes, that's right, for many years during the investigation Der-Yeghiayan had deep suspicions that pizza-loving, quiche-making, cat-loving Mark was really the Dread Pirate Roberts.

Ulbricht initially pleaded not guilty to seven charges. Before he was sentenced, parents of victims who had died of overdoses from drugs allegedly purchased on Silk Road said that their children would never have died if Silk Road didn't exist.

"The stated purpose [of Silk Road] was to be beyond the law. In the world you created over time, democracy didn't exist. You were captain of the ship; the Dread Pirate Roberts. You made your own laws," the judge told Ulbricht as she read the sentence.

He was sentenced to life in prison without parole in a New York courtroom on Friday, May 29, 2015.

Was the sentence fair? I don't know. If Ulbricht really did all the things he was accused of doing, maybe yes. But as far as the drug deaths? I have doubts. When people choose to take drugs, they know the risks. Can you hold him responsible for that? Do we hold the major pharmaceutical companies responsible for overdosing on the opioids they've been pushing for years? Not to my recollection.

Some have argued that the quality of the drugs sold on Silk Road was better than what was available on the street because of the feedback/rating system in place, and that Silk Road actually saved lives. That is also a valid point.

Until taking on the mantle of the Dread Pirate Roberts, Ulbricht was an extremely polite and well-educated young man who was a little clumsy with girls, which is why his closest friends were extremely surprised when they learned of his activities in what seemed like a parallel universe. Everybody thought: "How could this young man, who got along with everyone, end up becoming America's public enemy number one in such a short period of time?"

Although the preponderance of evidence suggests that Ulbricht was the creator of Silk Road and was the Dread Pirate Roberts, his supporters contend that he's innocent. Some in the Bitcoin community believe that, even if he actually was DPR, he had committed no real crime. Roger

Ver, aka Bitcoin Jesus, is an ex-convict himself and a staunch supporter of Ross Ulbricht. He donated around $165,000 to Ulbricht's legal defense.

Bitcoin Jesus believes that Ulbricht has committed no sins, that he was simply helping people get what they wanted out of life:

> He wasn't using any violence on anybody. The indictment doesn't say Ross Ulbricht smuggled drugs; what he did [was provide] a platform that allowed other people to buy and sell drugs. By the same exact logic, should we charge cell phone companies because a lot of drug deals have been done by people talking on cell phones. What about the internet as a whole? Or email providers? All these services enable people to buy and sell drugs and smuggle narcotics.

For Ver, the government's logic was crazy on multiple levels. He insisted that good people break bad laws. In the US, it was once illegal to help enslaved people escape into the North. Good people broke those laws, he said. He not only thought of Ulbricht as an innocent man, but also as a sort of libertarian hero:

> My point of view is that none of this would have ever happened if it wasn't for the government's insane war on drugs. If governments respected each individual's self-ownership, and allowed them to actually control their own bodies, drugs like these would be sold by CVS, Walgreens, or Amazon.com. There would have never been a need for the Silk Road, and none of the problems related to it would have ever happened.

(Note: Bitcoin Jesus must have been a hell of a good person, because he was breaking his own fair share of laws. He was found hiding in Spain in April 2024 and was subsequently indicted for evading US taxes—a cool $50 million worth. IRS Special Agent Tigran Gambaryan was part of this investigation. Small world! Bitcoin Jesus is now in the process of being extradited back to the United States, no crucifix necessary.)

A curious interview exists with another man claiming to be the real DPR. The interview was published in *Forbes* magazine in August 2013 and was titled, "An Interview With A Digital Drug Lord: The Silk Road's Dread Pirate Roberts." It was the only purported interview given by the man behind Silk Road, conducted by journalist Andy Greenberg. In the Q & A, Dread Pirate Roberts said he took over the site from its creator—which could have meant that he was not Ross Ulbricht. Or was it Ulbricht pretending not to be himself?

Over the course of five hours on July 4, 2013, DPR answered questions all routed through Tor and the Silk Road messaging system. When the journalist asked him why he started Silk Road, his answer was: "I didn't start the Silk Road, my predecessor did. From what I understand, it was an original idea to combine bitcoin and Tor to create an anonymous market. Everything was in place, he just put the pieces together."

The prosecution reportedly did not want the jury to see this interview during the trial of Ulbricht. Was it Ross Ulbricht, already trying to distance himself from his own work? Had Silk Road taken on a life of its own after Ulbricht had created it, much like how Satoshi Nakamoto created Bitcoin and then seemingly vanished into cyberspace?

Could there be any truth to the theory that Mark Karpelès was the real Dread Pirate Roberts, the person who actually ran Silk Road?

Will the real Dread Pirate Roberts please stand up?

He probably won't. He's probably hanging out at a sushi bar with Satoshi Nakamoto somewhere.

CHAPTER SEVEN

The Ides of February

During the Silk Road investigation, while the US was attempting to dismantle the site, Mark and Mt. Gox continued to prosper. Mark was doing interviews with documentary filmmakers; he was filmed espousing the merits of bitcoin while sitting on a bouncy exercise ball in his office to reporters. He was a minor celebrity, in and out of Japan.

By the middle of 2013, Mt. Gox was handling millions of dollars a day in transactions, sometimes as much as $20 million in a single day. As we know from the wisdom of Uncle Ben from Spiderman, "With great power comes great responsibility." Unfortunately, Mark had always loved Japanese manga and had relatively little interest in Western comics—so perhaps he was never exposed to this bit of comic-book wisdom. For Karpelès, with great power came great money, and with great money, great silliness. He let work consume him, and barely paid attention to his wife and his young son. She left him, and Japan, and Mark seemed to be shell-shocked.

He contemplated going after her and winning her back, but that would have meant leaving Mt. Gox behind for days or possibly weeks; as the company's Chief Executive Officer, Chief Financial Officer, and Chief Information Technology Officer, that just wasn't possible. At least not in his mind.

If he had learned to separate his personal account from that of his company, and simply paid for things out of his own lavish salary, things might have gone better down the line.

Young Mark, with his newfound wealth, went on a shopping spree that could generously be described as ill-advised. He began to indulge himself, splurging on pet projects, gratuitously expensive items (including a 6-million-yen bed), and other amusements. He reportedly spent around 20 million yen—roughly $166,000—on credit-card purchases and women, the latter of which seemed to take up most of his time and nearly all of his judgment. The Japanese tabloids were quick to point out that Mark had a certain preference for prostitutes, a detail they claimed came from the police.

He often lamented to friends about his wife leaving him, though he seemed to recover remarkably fast, diving headfirst into his newfound passions. But perhaps his most remarkable trait—if one could call it that—was his ability to ejaculate with an almost superhuman force. During one encounter, with a woman dressed in a furry cat costume, Mark's orgasm was apparently so powerful that his sperm shot across the room, hitting the six-million-yen bed he'd bought and leaving a permanent white stain on the siding. The bed was likely devalued by a million yen or so just from the incident.

Of course, as Mt. Gox began to grow, a stained bed would become the least of Mark's worries. With the expansion of the company and with the problems this created, 2012 had been a busy year. By November, to tackle business operations in North America, Mt. Gox signed a contract with a Silicon Valley–based Bitcoin service called CoinLab in order to manage the complex legal situation regarding Bitcoin regulatory business-related licenses in the United States.

In February 2013, Mt. Gox and CoinLab announced their partnership. CoinLab was relatively new on the scene, but they had gained attention due to the large amount of funding they had received—over half a million dollars from venture capitalists. They also managed the Bitcoin Foundation. The contract was such that CoinLab would handle all of Mt. Gox's services and clients in North America. It was a great deal for both parties. CoinLab had a small but passionate team that could use the clients and advice from an experienced company such as Mt. Gox. Mt. Gox, with CoinLab managing its US and Canadian clients, wouldn't need to bother with getting a license to function in the US.

Or so they thought. In fact, four different financial experts found four different answers to the question of whether a license was needed at all. Some said that Bitcoin was not regulated, thus a license would be unnecessary. Another said a license was required, but it would be nearly impossible to get one. For example, the Money Transmitting Business (MTB) license covering all US states cost almost $50 million to acquire. Mt. Gox didn't have $50 million to invest right away.

CoinLab said they could handle the pesky "license" situation.

A March 2013 ruling from the Financial Crimes Enforcement Network (FinCEN), an agency within the US Department of the Treasury, appeared to indicate that all money-transmitting businesses using virtual currencies had to get an MTB license. The guidance defined the circumstances under which virtual currency users could be categorized as money services businesses (also commonly known as money-transmitting businesses, or MTBs). MTBs must enforce Anti-Money Laundering (AML) and Know Your Client (KYC) measures, and identify the people that they do business with. The concern about Bitcoin and currency exchanges being used for crime was a concern that Mark shared. He had proactively contacted the Department of Justice (DOJ) on several occasions after the Silk Road story broke. The anti-money-laundering practices at Mt. Gox, which refused certain clients upon checking their fake passports, had kept out many Silk Road vendors as early as 2011.

In a letter sent via Federal Express to the DEA on June 10, 2011, and received by the agency on June 13, 2011, Karpelès wrote:

> We are a Japanese securities exchange known as Mt. Gox. [We are] contacting you in light of the recent media excitement surrounding Bitcoin. It has been brought to our immediate attention that there are US senators calling for quick and firm action from the DEA to shut down illegal narcotic and international drug trafficking services that are facilitated by a website known as the 'Silk Road.' Firstly, we would like you to be aware that we do not condone the use or trafficking of illegal substances, nor does our Bitcoin exchange directly or indirectly endorse the use of such services. Ultimately, we are pursuing a goal of accepted legitimacy, both for Bitcoin and our exchange. We are more than willing to comply with any

court-sanctioned investigations regarding our services.

We invite you to contact us.

In addition, Mark had set in place security safeguards so that stolen bitcoins couldn't be deposited or moved out of Mt. Gox. When a Bitcoin exchange was hacked and bitcoins were stolen, the stolen coins could be tracked on the blockchain. Mark didn't want any part in laundering them, so he set in place a system to make sure that didn't happen. He felt that there was almost a brotherhood of Bitcoin exchanges.

"An attack on one of us is an attack on all of us," he would say, echoing lines from the comic book *The Watchmen*. Those acts of kindness and altruism were measures that he would, in a way, be rewarded for later. Mt. Gox was not Silk Road—that was clear.

Meanwhile, in the US, one DEA special agent working on the Silk Road case seemed to have a rather unusual interest in Mt. Gox: Carl Mark Force IV, pseudonym Nob, who you'll remember for his fake murder of Curtis Green, for which he got paid in bitcoins.

Special Agent Force also was quite a fan of Bitcoin. In fact, he and his partner Bridges had accounts at Mt. Gox. The question that any Internal Affairs investigators at either of their agencies should have been asking was: how on earth did two special agents on a federal salary have so many bitcoins in their accounts?

Force apparently had enough bitcoins and bitcoin savvy to try to contact Mark. On April 8, 2013, Force reached out to Mark through a LinkedIn invitation. The message even mentioned that he was a DEA special agent. Even after being ignored, Force attempted on multiple occasions to partner up with Mark.

While Force was trying to cuddle up to Mark, there was more trouble on the horizon. On May 2, CoinLab filed a $75 million lawsuit against Mt. Gox. According to the lawsuit, Mt. Gox hadn't given CoinLab access to their North American clients and had continued to serve its customers in North America.

Force saw the news as an opportunity for himself. On May 7, he offered to become the representative of Mt. Gox in North America. His email said: "I saw the news yesterday that you won't be partnering with CoinLab. Sorry to hear that. If you are still looking for a US and Canada representative, please keep me in mind. Thank you very much," and the email was signed "Carl Force."

In mid-May 2013, a total of $5 million was suddenly seized from Mt. Gox North America's Wells Fargo Dwolla account and Mark Karpelès's private account by the Department of Homeland Security. There was no warning, and no one knew exactly why. Ostensibly, the warrant had been issued because Mt. Gox had failed to register as a money transmitter, putting them in violation of the new FinCEN guidelines.

On May 14, 2013, Force wrote to Mark: "Told you, you should have partnered with me!".

Mark had no idea what was really going on, but the $5 million freeze was financial frostbite. Things got worse. "CoinLab threatened Mt. Gox legally, and then Mizuho Bank started to say that it would be great if Mt. Gox could find another bank. Then a few weeks later, they started to refuse handling of any outgoing international remittance transactions," Mark recalled sadly. "Because we didn't have a better alternative, we started to use Japan Post Bank to do our computer transfers, at a maximum of ten per day, while our lawyers in the US were discussing with the prosecutors whether they could cancel the fund seizure."

However, using Japan Post Bank wasn't easy. Many transactions had to be done in cash. At one point, Mt. Gox employees were walking in and out of the offices with paper bags full of tens of thousands of dollars in cash.

The federal seizure of Mt. Gox funds made everyone wary of Bitcoin once again, but Mt. Gox was still in control of the vast majority of all bitcoin transactions. Mt. Gox employees said that the company eventually created a working relationship with Japan Net Bank to solve their money-transfer issues domestically.

All of this collective chaos meant that Mark was unable to attend a phenomenally important event held in San Jose, California, which was also the inaugural conference of the Bitcoin Foundation. Roger Ver was there, and so were the Winklevoss twins, who had helped create Facebook (in a way). They owned 1 percent of all the bitcoins in the world at that point. Mark should have been there, but it was impossible for him to go. Everyone noticed that he wasn't present.

A few weeks after the seizure, the documentary filmmakers responsible for *The Rise and Rise of Bitcoin* paid a visit to the Mt. Gox offices and interviewed Mark. We were told they agreed with Mark not to discuss the seizure.

It's a film worth watching even now, as it captures the early days of the cryptocurrency frenzy. Mark and his Chief Marketing Officer, Gonzague Gay-Bouchery, show the filmmakers around the relatively new offices as they explain that they are reaching 100,000 new customers per month. Mark gives them a tour of the office where eighteen people are working in a tastefully decorated open-office space. Most of the office workers are seated on plush chairs in front of MacBook computers, high-tech Dyson fans are placed strategically around the room, and, for reasons unknown, stuffed rabbits with red bow ties are sitting on the desks of several employees.

Mark sits at a desk facing away from everyone, but still in the same open space. At the time, as well as holding the positions of CEO, CFO, CTO, he is the lead developer. He happily discusses his favorite programming languages, and walks the filmmakers into the data center and server room, where photography is prohibited. Mark brags that with new system optimization, he can go from 100 orders per second to 100 million orders per second. He is the picture of confidence.

He even takes the time to show off his other keyboarding skills—playing the electronic piano. It is, unfortunately, not a dazzling performance.

Yes, there were problems. Yet, by all accounts, Mt. Gox was a success. It was still the largest Bitcoin exchange. It traded an average of $6 million a day, which was 76 percent of all Bitcoin transactions.

This wasn't enough. Mark wanted more. He wanted to set up a coffee shop that accepted Bitcoin to attract more Japanese users and so people could see how it worked. It would also act as a community center for Bitcoin fans.

In August 2013, Mark launched the Bitcoin Café project. In September, he bought the computer software-modeling company Shade3D, allegedly in order to have a side business and to guarantee the availability of cash flow in case he needed it.

But while Mark worked on his café project, Bitcoin was constantly in the news overseas.

On October 1, the FBI arrested Ross Ulbricht, the alleged Silk Road founder. That same month, Mt. Gox acquired a Money Service Operator License in Hong Kong. On October 29, the Las Vegas startup Robocoin launched the world's first Bitcoin ATM.

In November 2013, the Bitcoin price exceeded $1,000 on Mt. Gox. In December, the number of verified customers on the exchange surpassed one million.

Despite his wealth, Mark was spending most of his free time eating junk food and watching anime while his code was compiling. As his friend and colleague Julien Laglasse, a Frenchman living in Tokyo, said, "Mark was happy as long as he had a pizza, a coke, a computer to work on, and his two cats around him. He was not a greedy guy." Mt. Gox was becoming successful, and as Mark was managing millions of dollars of clients' money, the problem was that he didn't care enough about money. Nonetheless, Mark was moving up in the world—figuratively and literally. Mark moved to the twenty-eighth floor of the luxurious apartment complex *La Tour Aobadai*, due to domestic problems with his ex-wife, Kyoko.

January saw him rise above the crowd, but February would be his downfall.

What should have been a small problem for Mt. Gox became the spark that consumed the company. In the beginning of February 2014, someone on the IRC chat #mtgox publicly announced that Mt. Gox could be attacked via the method known as "transaction malleability," and explained how to do it. As a consequence of the warning, Mark decided to block the attack immediately. After a short battle and some sweating, he found a way to make it impossible: a blockade on the withdrawals allowed him to stop that form of attack for the time being. Then there were veiled threats. Mark ignored them.

On February 7, Mt. Gox halted all Bitcoin transactions until a workaround was found. Were the withdrawals halted due to the theft or disappearance of hundreds of thousands of bitcoins owned by Mt. Gox customers, as well as Mt. Gox itself, or was the reason the discovery of transaction malleability? In any event, Mark decided the easiest way to stop the leak was to stop withdrawals.

People became very worried.

As Mark struggled to fix the system glitch, he did a reconciling of accounts. He compared the amount of money Mt. Gox had in its hot wallet (the cash register of sorts for the company) to the amount of money it had in cold storage (the equivalent of a bank safe). There was a tremendous amount of bitcoin gone. Mt. Gox had a serious problem.

On February 15, Mark informed one of his trusted employees that an estimated 850,000 bitcoins were unaccounted for—at the time, worth close to $500 million. The employee was told that the bitcoins had possibly been siphoned off over several months by users exploiting flaws in the system. In particular, there seemed to be a systems glitch that had made it possible to get a payment reissued. The former employee told me that because the firm hadn't hired an accounting firm or an auditor to keep the books, the theft had gone undetected.

Teikoku Databank, Japan's largest and most respected credit-rating agency, had reviewed the company in July 2013. The bank had given it a D4, the worst possible rating a company can receive on their scale. One of the reasons for the low rating was the lack of qualified accounting staff at the company.

Mt. Gox had survived hacks, system failures, and seizures from the authorities—but now, things looked hopeless for them. Thousands of customers were unable to withdraw their deposits, and Karpelès wasn't talking to the press. He wasn't speaking to anyone. He was more or less in hiding. Speculation ran rampant as to what exactly had happened, and the Bitcoin world went into a panic.

In front of his office on a snowy day, Mark had an encounter with angry Mt. Gox user Kolin Burges. He had flown all the way from England to find out what was going on. He would later become the symbol and angry voice of all Mt. Gox users. He was clad in a black woolen hat, scarf, and long black jacket, and, wielding his handheld sign, confronted Mark while cameras filmed it all.

"Do you still have everyone's bitcoins?" he said, blocking Mark's path.

Mark, with a frappuccino in his hand, dodged and weaved, trying to get into the building. He told Burges, frustrated, "I'm going to call the police."

Kolin responded, "Go for it. I'm not touching you. I haven't touched you ... Do you still have everyone's bitcoins?"

Mark didn't answer. He could only say, "Don't come inside, please."

He didn't have the bitcoins. And that was the problem.

He didn't have enough money to keep the operation afloat

either. The $5 million worth of frozen assets in the United States would have helped, but, of course, that money was untouchable.

Key members of the Mt. Gox staff and consultants gathered and brainstormed for a way to keep the company solvent, protect its assets, and move forward. They drafted a document entitled "Crisis Strategy Draft" that was meant to lay the problems out to investors and work out solutions.

This document was only shown to a handful of people, including the Winklevoss twins, who were active investors in the industry and other executives. A few days after being drafted, it was leaked to the blogger the Two-Bit Idiot, who published it on the web on Monday February 24 at 6.23 pm New York time. It spread across the internet in hours. The press was soon all over the story, including Nathalie and me.

"At this point, our last-minute efforts to discreetly refinance the company and avoid insolvency had pretty much been sabotaged," a former employee told me.

Mt. Gox had suspended all trading after internal investigations discovered a loss of as many as 744,408 bitcoins. Mark had been hoping that, somehow, the firm could still be saved. But the accounting practices at the firm were so haphazard that even what seemed like "an exact amount" wasn't exact. On February 25, after confirming with their lawyers that the end was near, the Mt. Gox site was shut down entirely.

What the hell had happened? There were theories galore.

Jason Maurice, the former chief hacker at *WizSec*, who currently works as a freelance security advisor, believed that Mark misunderstood the severity of the security issue and didn't implement a correct fix when it was found. "He basically dismissed a multimillion-dollar bug in his software that any decent software engineer would have immediately realized was a huge issue. Any financial institution would have a huge quality assurance team to find such bugs, but for Karpelès, it was all up to him."

In addition to leaking money through the bug, the company might have accidentally thrown away bitcoins. "It is hard to believe this level of incompetence," Maurice said.

This really shouldn't have surprised anyone who knew Mark. You wouldn't want to put a guy in charge of cyber security who forgets his laptop on a park bench in Tokyo and expects to get it back.

The bitcoins had been poorly secured, digitally and physically. The exchange claimed that they stored about 90 percent of their bitcoins in paper wallets and USB keys. A paper wallet is just the name for a printed document that contains all the necessary data to generate one or more private keys. By moving the bitcoins into a paper wallet, the key is no longer digitally stored anywhere, and thus not subject to attacks by hackers. However, if the paper wallet—basically a sheet of paper—is lost, the bitcoins stored in the wallet are also lost. According to former employees, who spoke to me after the collapse, paper wallets at Mt. Gox were oftentimes haphazardly stored in the office, buried in sofas, and pushed behind desks. Mark denied this when I asked him about it.

According to another former employee who spoke to me after the collapse, Mt. Gox "rented safety-deposit boxes in banks. When they needed to refill the transaction accounts, they took the bitcoins out of storage and deposited them into the system. There was no reconciliation in the accounting sense between the cold storage and the transactions done. As long as money was coming in at a steady pace, no one realized that actually they had been losing huge amounts of bitcoin. And when they did—all hell broke loose."

Roughly four hours after our *Daily Beast* story was published online, Mt. Gox filed for bankruptcy protection with the Tokyo District Court. It declared liabilities of about $64 million at the time, and JPY 3.84 billion in assets. The company said it had lost almost 750,000 of its customers' bitcoins, and around 100,000 of its own bitcoins—roughly 850,000 bitcoins, totaling around 7 percent of all bitcoins, which were worth around $473 million near the time of the filing.

Mark remembers that day well, as he told me in an interview:

> I went to the Tokyo District Court with my lawyers in the afternoon and, by the end of the afternoon, the order was given. With just thirty minutes to prepare, we launched a press conference. The room was full.
>
> The press conference [in and of itself] went okay, although one cameraman decided to ask questions in English, which I was not prepared for. But the worst thing was the walk to the taxi outside, with all the reporters surrounding me, getting closer and closer to me. Once in the taxi, the driver had to struggle hard to get out of there. I was followed all the way to the Baker & McKenzie offices, where I finally could rest a bit before driving back home.

Mt. Gox released an official statement, saying that the bankruptcy was related to a "bug" in the Bitcoin software algorithm, which had been exploited by one or more persons who had "hacked" the Bitcoin network. Because the company had a business plan up to 2017, clearly with a plan for the future, some felt it was unlikely that its CEO had stolen his clients' money.

After filing for bankruptcy, Mark worked at his old office in Shibuya. The number of employees had been reduced drastically. The little coffee shop on the first floor that was supposed to turn into the world's first Bitcoin café never came into being. These days, it's just another co-working space.

What remains of that dream are Bitcoin Café coffee mugs, sitting in the cupboards of a few people in Japan. I have one of them. The mug is substantial, colored aqua blue, with the bitcoin symbol on one side in white lettering, and BITCOIN CAFÉ written underneath it in all-caps. I'm drinking Vietnamese coffee from it as I finish writing this book. It's a great coffee mug, made in Japan.

At the time of the bankruptcy, Yoshihide Suga, a top government spokesman—who would later become prime minister of Japan—stated that authorities, including the police and Japan's Financial Services Agency, were collecting information on the bitcoin trade in Japan and considering regulatory action. For those individuals with bitcoins trapped in the Mt. Gox system—some with as much as $150,000 worth—whatever regulatory action that did come would probably come too late. In addition, there were reports that US authorities had begun investigating Mt. Gox. and had subpoenaed individuals who had worked for or still worked for the company.

Karl-Friedrich Lenz, professor of German and European law at Aoyama Gakuin University in Tokyo, and author of the academic paper "Legal Issue of the New Internet Currency Bitcoin in EU Law and German Law," said he believes that Mt. Gox should have been treated as a banking institution and not allowed to operate without a license under current Japanese law:

> If Mt. Gox had been treated like a bank, this problem would have never happened. It would have had to have proper accounting and people with financial skills to get licensed. It is unlikely that the Japanese government would have granted such authority to a company run by a twenty-seven-year-old computer genius with no financial background.

Mark recalls that, in the days following the bankruptcy announcement, things calmed down and the trustee appointed by the Tokyo District Court began figuring out what to do. "We had to rapidly put in place a call-center, which I developed within a couple of hours, the best I could, and then a lot of things started to move along."

He had to be available at any time to answer questions from the American liquidator. He was hoping for a civil rehabilitation of the company, but unfortunately, ran into problems due to his inability to travel outside Japan. This further doomed Mt. Gox to the scrap heap.

In the US, his lawyers filed a "Chapter 15," which is done when a liquidation procedure or a rehabilitation process is taking place in another country. As part of routine procedure, the US courts asked to meet with Karpelès in order to ask him questions; otherwise; the filing would be impossible, and the assets of the company in the US would be threatened with seizure.

> A rumor went around saying that I was planning to travel to the US, which triggered FinCEN to submit a subpoena, and the DHS dispatched two agents in each airport that could let me inside the US. I had become a PoI, a person of interest. Of course, it was out of question for me to travel to the US under such conditions. And the court in Tokyo didn't allow me to leave the country without the guarantee that the US would allow me to travel back to Japan. So Japan refused to proceed to rehabilitation, and began liquidating around the end of April 2014. After that, I tried to make Tibanne, my first company, work, but without great success. By the end of the summer, I met a Swiss reporter who became obsessed with finding the missing Bitcoins.

> That reporter was Nathalie Stucky.

On March 20, 2014, Mark discovered an old paper wallet containing 200,000 bitcoins. This was a tremendously good thing, as it would later turn out, but at the time it raised suspicions. This was good news and bad news. People wondered: if Mt. Gox could simply misplace or lose 200,000 bitcoins, maybe they had lost them all. Maybe Mark was hiding them.

There are many mysteries remaining. Independent investigators started focusing on how the purchase of Mt. Gox took place between Mark Karpelès and Jed McCaleb.

Some believe that the theft of the bitcoins took place during the period when transfers to paper wallets were occurring. If so, the theft occurred precisely when it would have been the hardest moment to detect.

After the bankruptcy of Mt. Gox, Mark's lawyers went to the Japanese police and filed a report requesting that they look into the hacking of the company and the theft of the missing bitcoins. The police opened an investigation.

Some cybercrime experts believed that the Japanese police didn't have the skills to solve the case. In fact, because confidence in the Japanese police was low, some Mt. Gox creditors launched an independent probe. Karpelès, however, thought that those who launched the independent initiative had underestimated the Japanese police. The police were making progress in their investigation on the lost bitcoins and cash, he believed. He didn't have all the details, but he had more details than most. This was because he was cooperating with the police as much as he could. In the early summer of 2014, when discussing the progress of the investigation with Ms. Stucky and me, he was optimistic.

> I have seen things that others will never see. And, based on that, I think the Japanese police are quite efficient. But I totally support the idea that several people start their own independent investigations. It is generally a good idea to have different people having different ways of looking into the same problem. The police do not report in detail on what they are doing. That's why it might seem like they are not doing anything, but they are actually working on this. It is, however, a recurrent problem and a fact that the Japanese police arrest innocent people and make them

confess to crimes that they didn't commit. So, I simply hope that they won't anything crazy. There's no guarantee, of course … Personally, I support their efforts to find the culprit or the culprits. The method used is less important to me than the result.

Mark would find out that those methods could be quite cruel, and that the results would be nothing like he had imagined. But as the police continued their investigation, the world would learn that across the ocean, the US authorities had been continuing another investigation: the question of whether or not Mark Karpelès was really the Dread Pirate Roberts.

Everyone, including me, was looking at Mark with a great deal of suspicion. Even if he wasn't Dread Pirate Roberts, was Mark Karpelès a victim or a criminal?

CHAPTER EIGHT

The unusual suspects

There was an American situation comedy TV show called *Everybody Loves Raymond*, about the wacky daily life of a successful sports columnist and his dysfunctional family, which screened from 1996 to 2005. If Mark had been given his own reality show in 2014, the title would have been *Everybody Hates Mark*. It would have been the wacky tragi-comic story of a once-successful cyber entrepreneur and all his angry friends, creditors, and the people who wanted to see him dead or in jail. Mark would definitely have been the comic relief, with his goofy smile and sometimes amazingly delayed reactions.

Mark had few friends left, and enemies galore.

On February 24, 2014, one day before Mt. Gox went blank, he received an email from a person operating under the name "Carpenoctem" who wanted to extort money from Mark, warning him that "angry Silk Road vendors were acting against Mt. Gox."

Nathalie Stucky did a lengthy interview with Mark in 2014. It paints a picture of a very lonely and lost Mark. It also shows a Mark aware of his own failings:

Q: What are the things that you desire the most today?
A: I would like to be less lonely. That could mean different things, but a big problem I have is that I don't have many people who understand me, and it isn't always easy. I am not a very social person, I used to be worse, but now I learned how to detect the flaws I have and I am more capable of interacting with people.
Q: What do you think life gave you? And what did people give you?
A: Until now, I think I was really lucky, because not many people can have the same things that I do. And at the same time, I think I am unlucky when I look at how it all ended, it's actually quite horrible. And I really hope we are going to find out what really happened.

As Mark tried to figure out what the hell had happened, so did the police. So did investigative journalists. So did a team of independent investigators.

Kim Nilsson, a humble and soft-spoken Swedish software engineer, lost approximately twelve bitcoins in the collapse of Mt. Gox, making him one of the least to suffer, but he was pissed off in his own slow-burning fashion. He comes across as a younger version of Santa Claus, a more stoic Kris Kringle, with a sharp, analytical mind. He didn't know anything about the blockchain when Mt. Gox collapsed, but his learning curve was steep. He, Jason Maurice, and a few other dudes who'd lost out when Mt. Gox went south got together to get to the bottom of the mystery. They formed a company, WizSec, a blockchain security firm. They were going to prove their mettle by solving the half-billion-dollar mystery: where, when, and how had those bitcoins vanished, and who had them?

"Of course, I had my suspicions that Mark Karpelès might be behind it all," he remembers.

All of us suspected that Mark may have been the real culprit.

Since the shutdown of Mt. Gox, the Bitcoin community and press had vilified Mark Karpelès as a clown and conman. Japanese tabloid magazines portrayed him as a "beast" hiding in his "dungeon." Mark was called an oaf, a terrible businessman, and "someone who should have never run a company." He was besieged with death threats, every day.

His reputation was damaged further when, as the New Year kicked off in 2015, the Silk Road trial began. In a Manhattan federal courtroom, Ross Ulbricht's lawyer immediately tried to peg Karpelès as the real Dread Pirate Roberts.

Ulbricht, as you know, was eventually charged with drug trafficking, criminal enterprise, aiding and abetting the distribution of drugs over the internet, computer hacking, and money laundering, and faced a lifetime in prison. During cross-examination, DHS Special Agent Jared Der-Yeghiayan said he had pursued Mark as the suspected owner and operator of Silk Road.

His investigation of Mark even led to conflict within Homeland Security Investigations (HSI). During the trial, Der-Yeghiayan was asked, "What you had concluded was that Mark was essentially behind Silk Road but that his associate Ashley Barr was Dread Pirate Roberts?"

He responded, "The things [Karpelès] would write online did not match the level of English skills that Dread Pirate Roberts possessed. So, I thought it was someone else close to him, and there was a person that shared some of the same viewpoints that was working for him by the name of Ashley Barr."

You may remember that while Der-Yeghiayan monitored Mark from Chicago, an HSI team in Baltimore seized roughly $5 million from a Mt. Gox subsidiary in May 2013. The real reasons they seized the money wouldn't be known until after Ulbricht's trial. At the time, the Department of Homeland Security claimed Mark was running an unlicensed and illegal money-transfer business.

Der-Yeghiayan reportedly believed the Baltimore division had dropped the ball on proving Karpelès was the owner of Silk Road. He wrote an angry email to fellow DHS staffers protesting the Baltimore agents' activities.

In fact, Karpelès was open with American authorities. He actually notified them when he discovered over 100 fake American passports being used to set up Mt. Gox accounts. He also acknowledged owning a hosting service used by part of the Silk Road network. "Part of the Silk Road network, silkroadmarket.org, was using a hosting service that I still owned," he notes.

However, with Ulbricht's defense lawyer Joshua Dratel trying to claim that Mark was the evil mastermind behind Silk Road, we had to ask him if it was true for the article we were writing. Frankly, I turned red out of shame while writing him the email. They say there are no stupid questions, but sometimes there are. Fortunately, Mark had a witty answer to our stupid question. He'd lost everything, but he still had his off-kilter sense of humor:

> This is probably going to be disappointing for you, but I am not Dread Pirate Roberts. The investigation reached that conclusion already—this is why I am not the one sitting during the Silk Road trial, and I can only feel sad for defense attorney Joshua Dratel trying everything he can to point the attention away from his client.
>
> I have nothing to do with Silk Road and do not condone what has been happening there. I believe Bitcoin [and its underlying technology] is not meant to help people evade the law, but to improve everyone's way of life by offering never-thought-of-before possibilities.

Karpelès expressed concern that revealing too much about his knowledge of the Silk Road investigation could place former employees and others in danger. Following repeated attempts to ask him if he was the Silk Road founder, Karpelès repeated, with some mirth, "I'm not a pirate nor a fraudster. Nor, for the record, am I the creator of Bitcoin, the elusive Satoshi Nakamoto."

I hit up a few sources to see where the idea that Mark was really DPR had come from and when that idea had been shelved.

Sources close to the DHS told us that Karpelès had been eliminated as a suspect by the end of 2013 and that he had been relatively cooperative with the government. The sources added that they believed some of his clients were involved in running the website. The DHS also hinted that a corrupt investigator on the US side had pointed to Karpelès as the culprit as well. Dread Pirate Roberts had desperately tried to reach Karpelès many times months after the Silk Road investigation began.

On Sept 1, 2013, exactly one month before Ulbricht's arrest, Dread Pirate Roberts sent several emails to Karpelès with the header "info regarding active law enforcement investigation." The emails were sent to Karpelès' bitcoinfoundation.org address. The email read:

> Greetings Mark
> As the subject says, I have some information for you as well as a special request. I don't want to say any more without PGP protection. Do you have a public key I could use?

Mark didn't respond to any of the emails because he never used his bitcoinfoundation.org email. Dread Pirate Roberts didn't stop trying to contact Mark, probably because he believed that Mark was working with US law enforcement and aiding their investigation into the Silk Road. And that was true.

Mark, it turns out, was an informant for the investigation and had proactively contacted the Department of Justice (DOJ) on several occasions. The anti-money-laundering practices at Mt. Gox, which refused certain clients upon checking their fake passports, had kept out many Silk Road vendors as early as 2011.

As mentioned before, Mt. Gox refused to open accounts for individuals with fake passports, and did basic due diligence on all their clients.

Mark was working with the good guys, and someone had tipped off Dread Pirate Roberts about it. In the uncensored version of Ulbricht's journal, Ross wrote that the entity he called "French Maid" claimed Mark gave information about Dread Pirate Roberts to the DHS (Department of Homeland Security).

It seems that Dread Pirate Roberts knew Karpelès had been cooperating with the investigation, but he didn't know how much the authorities knew about his operation—and that was what he wanted to know, needed to know.

The journal was submitted as evidence at Ulbricht's trial. There was a notation on September 13, 2013, in which Ulbricht offered $100,000 for information about the joint investigation. A day later, Dread Pirate Roberts paid $100,000 to someone called "French Maid". It was obvious that the prosecution was unhappy about the existence of French Maid. Was there a leak in the investigation?

The prosecution redacted almost all information about Dread Pirate Roberts buying information from law-enforcement sources when they presented evidence to the jury. But they had made a colossal screw-up. While they censored the pdfs, they forgot to redact embedded information in other files, making it possible to read the whole journal. Journalists and investigators rejoiced. There was enough information there to allow people to figure out how to access the many email accounts of Dread Pirate Roberts and to see the evidence for themselves.

So, who was French Maid? Karpelès had some idea—he remembered the odd email from Carl Mark Force, the DEA agent.

On March 30, 2015, *after* Ulbricht had been found guilty, the DOJ released documents about two federal agents with lead roles in the investigation to take down Silk Road. They had allegedly stolen proceeds from the underground site in the form of bitcoins. They hid their illicit earnings while conducting the investigations.

For all of us following the Silk Road trial, this was huge news. These two rogue federal agents had played a huge role in fucking up the life of Mark and had indirectly hastened the decline of Mt. Gox.

Of course, what also struck everyone as unfair was that the fact that agents working on the Silk Road case had been arrested on criminal charges was only made public *after* the Silk Road trial had concluded. The DOJ had more or less covered it up.

I called *The Daily Beast*, and worked with the correspondent who had been covering the Silk Road trial to put all the pieces together. Here is what we were able to figure out after reading through piles of documents and affidavits, and talking to sources.

US law enforcement sources confirmed that one of the agents leaked information about Mark Karpelès to the Silk Road operators. The agents revealed that Karpelès cooperated with their investigation on several occasions. The agents also tried to extort funds from Mt. Gox. They demanded that Mt. Gox do business with them, but Mt. Gox refused. In response to that, the US government had seized a total of $5 million from the company's US accounts.

According to court documents and government sources, former DEA Special Agent Carl Mark Force IV, who was arrested on April 30, 2015, had allegedly asked Ross Ulbricht to pay him $250,000 in bitcoins not to disclose information to the government. Force also allegedly gave information that

Karpelès had shared with authorities to Ulbricht in exchange for money.

US federal court documents outlining the charges against the two agents also allege that former Secret Service employee Shaun Bridges stole more than $800,000 in bitcoins from Mt. Gox during the investigation into Silk Road. He allegedly wired the funds from a Mt. Gox account that he controlled to a personal investment account over the course of nine transfers from March 6 to May 7, 2013, just days before seizing Mt. Gox's US funds.

In other words, Mt. Gox had its account frozen on the orders of two Special Agents with ulterior motives. Carl Force was pissed off that Mark wouldn't become his business partner. Bridges wanted to cover up the money flowing into his accounts. Mark had been punished for doing the right thing.

We had to consider the possibility that maybe these two bad cops had stolen the remaining unaccounted-for 650,000 bitcoins. It seemed unlikely, but not impossible.

Speaking of punishment, this was what happened to the dynamic duo.

The full scope of Force and Bridges' corruption remains a mystery. The government, eager to sweep the mess under the rug, struck plea deals with both agents, neatly tying up their cases without further public disclosures.

The agents—both of whom pleaded guilty and went to prison—were never compelled to decrypt their Silk Road chat logs, nor were they required to turn over their laptops, email accounts, or any other digital evidence that might have shed light on just how deeply they had been involved. Assistant US Attorney Kathryn Haun put it plainly at Bridges' sentencing:

"There are a lot of unanswered questions."

In 2016, more than a year after Ross Ulbricht's trial had concluded, the defense discovered critical evidence suggesting that someone within the government, someone with high-level access to Silk Road, had tampered with digital information used to convict Ross. Was it Bridges and Force? Another corrupt agent? Or someone else entirely?

But no one seems to know who had altered the evidence, or if they do know, they're not talking. And to this day, no one knows the full extent of how much Force and Bridges compromised the Silk Road website and the evidence against Ulbricht.

The prosecution of Force revealed him to be a sociopath among sociopaths. The words of Joshua Dratel, Ross's defense attorney, summed it up nicely, noting that Force had a special capacity "for fraud, deception, forgery, abuse of his government authority and access—including predatory and retaliatory conduct and false accusations against innocent [people—and inventing complex, layered cover stories to conceal his misdeeds."

In 2015, the court sentenced Force to six and a half years, and Bridges to six. But Bridges wasn't quite done—he tried to launder 1,606 stolen bitcoins that had slipped under the prosecutor's radar. He earned himself an extra two years for that one.

By 2020, both corrupt agents had served their time. Force walked free in October of that year, having done five and a half years. A year later, in October 2021, Bridges followed, after serving his six-year term. Meanwhile, Ross Ulbricht remains behind bars, entering his fifteenth year of a double-life sentence, plus forty years, without parole.

Mark told us in an email: "The fact that information provided by our lawyers to law enforcement ended up being known by parties being investigated [before arrest] is a very big issue. We shut out Silk Road vendors as far back as 2011," said Mark. "This could have led many parties, who might have held relevant information for law enforcement, to not share it out of fear for their business and/or their life."

Now Mark knew that DPR had wanted him dead. That didn't make him feel any better.

So, in The Great Bitcoin Heist, the suspects who might have stolen the bitcoins, based on motive alone, now included not only Mark, but possibly Dread Pirate Roberts, angry Silk Road vendors, and maybe even the cops tracking Dread Pirate Roberts. Yes, everybody hated Mark.

Well, maybe not everybody. Kim Nilsson had started off almost sure that Mark was involved in theft, but, as his analysis moved forward, he began to wonder. "It seemed to me that Mark wanted to know what really happened just as badly as we did," he said. Kim and his crew were able to get an invitation to Mark's new and downscaled apartment by offering to bring him the ingredients to bake his famous apple pie. Mark began feeding Kim not only food, but also the data he needed to figure it all out. In a way, Mark had a friend.

But Mark's troubles kept continuing. By early 2015, there were additional and new accusations against him that he couldn't laugh off. Around January 15, 2015, Bitcoin millionaire and Belgian tech entrepreneur Olivier Janssens publicly accused Mark Karpelès of having made death threats against one of his former employees when Mt. Gox was still in business.

Janssens, a former client of Mt. Gox, gained fame in late

January 2014 for becoming the first person to pay for a flight using bitcoins. He made some of his fortune through Mt. Gox at a time when the company was flourishing. Unfortunately, he claimed to have lost the equivalent of $5 million when Mt. Gox filed for bankruptcy.

In a tweet, Janssens wrote, "I have black on white proof of Mark Karpelès making multiple death threats against an ex-employee. So [do] Japanese police. #RossUlbricht." The accusation sparked a torrent of comments on social media.

It was likely that Janssens planned to give the "evidence" to Ulbricht's lawyer. Luckily for Mark, Judge Katherine B. Forrest ruled that Mark's involvement in Silk Road was speculative. She would not allow future testimony regarding Mark being Dread Pirate Roberts. Although this was good news for Mark, the fact he was mentioned in the trial, and was accused of making death threats, made him look even worse.

The evidence that Janssens planned to bring against Mark included emails allegedly sent by him to a former Mt. Gox employee. One email, dated Saturday March 1, 2014, read: "Keep in mind the warning letter you received. If you make any statements that contain confidential information, we will find a way to deal with it, maybe outside of the law, by making you return home as a dead man, for example. I'd appreciate it if you keep quiet. Thanks."

It was supposedly signed by Mark and sent from his email address. Mark allegedly sent a second threatening email a couple of days later, on Monday, March 3, which read: "We are watching you closely. Always remember that."

Threatening someone's life is a criminal offense in Japan that could be considered intimidation (*kyohaku*) or extortion (*kyokatsu*), depending on the details of the threat. However, in an odd turn of events, Janssens retracted his accusation and announced that his allegations were under investigation by experts on his own team. A cybersecurity expert close to Janssens admitted that the emails could have been forged by the recipient or even by a third party. Janssens' lawyer, Takaaki Nagashima, said he could not comment on the accusations, because the complaints had been made by a former Mt. Gox employee who was, like all the other former employees of Mt. Gox, a suspect in what might have been "an inside job."

Mark denied ever making death threats against his employees. He claimed to be confident that a forensic analysis of the emails would show that they had been forged.

In a written statement on January 20, 2015, Karpelès' lawyer in Tokyo, Nobuyasu Ogata, wrote that the accusations had no basis in fact. "There are individuals circulating amateurish forged documents as if they were real evidence, and we cannot overlook this."

The question remains: why would an ex-employee falsely claim to be receiving death threats from Mark? Could the ex-employee have taken the bitcoins and made false claims to throw people off the scent?

Who had looted Mt. Gox? There were so many possibilities. A rogue employee. Mark. Silk Road vendors. Special agents. A hacker. Dread Pirate Roberts. A hacker hired by Dread Pirate Roberts?

There were even suggestions floating around that a trading bot inside the Mt. Gox system known as Wily-Bot had malfunctioned and released all the coins over several years.

So that was another suspect—a rogue bot, possibly even a malfunctioning AI program installed in the Mt. Gox system.

Anything seemed possible. At that point in time, if you had asked me if Satoshi Nakamoto himself could be a suspect, I would have said: maybe.

Suspects? There were plenty of them. But as the clock struck midnight on January 1, 2015, and the *Yomiuri* newspaper screamed "Inside Job" in bold headlines about the Mt. Gox debacle, it became painfully clear that the police and prosecutors had already zeroed in on their man.

I should have seen it coming. I had written about the Japanese police doing an abysmal job of cyber investigations and arresting an innocent person in the recent past.

But it didn't matter. Mark Karpelès was the guilty party in their eyes.

CHAPTER NINE

And justice for none

I like to say I risked my life in order to keep my promise to look after things for Mark. In reality, I'm just deathly allergic to cats. And with Mark in jail for at least twenty-three days, I had to look after his cats, Tibane and Julia. They were left alone inside his house for about twenty-four hours before someone (me) was allowed to enter the house and feed them.

It required wading through an army of Japanese reporters parked in front of Mark's house, who were surprised and horrified to see a fellow reporter entering and leaving the suspect's house. In some effort at transparency, I tweeted pictures of myself and the cats.[*]

Someone had to take care of the cats. That job had landed on my shoulders.

---

[*] It was still called Twitter back then, not 'X', Elon Musk didn't own the platform, and he was more concerned about his hairline than right-wing conspiracy theories. Donald Trump hadn't been elected president of the United States yet.

Well, while I was not fond of cats, they were presumed innocent until proven guilty. Quickly, I convinced Nathalie to look after them; Nathalie was fine with the creatures. Then, for several days, Julien, his friend and colleague, went to his house to play with Mark's cats until finally deciding to adopt them. The public may not have been fond of Mark, but his cats seem to have had a fanbase because, in the midst of all of this, the cat tweets were very popular.

On September 11, 2015, Japanese prosecutors filed the first criminal charges against Mark. The alleged crime: embezzling over $2.7 million of his clients' money. The police had detained him, at that point, for more than forty days.

Mark's legal team at the Ogata Law Office in Tokyo said that the accusations of embezzlement were unfounded. His lawyers claimed that the money Mark was being accused of embezzling had actually been used for investments, on behalf of the company. The $2.7 million had come from his company's revenues, which had reached $28 million in total. The Tokyo-based certified accountant said that if the prosecutors were charging Mark with embezzlement for this amount of money, the majority of other businesses in Japan could be charged for the same crime.

The police strategy seemed to be to arrest him on minor charges and to serve him with warrants until he confessed to a larger crime. You can see what the cops were thinking: people accused of a crime are more likely to confess, even if they didn't do it. In one infamous case, a rogue hacker tricked the Japanese cyber cops into making four false arrests, and some of the accused made false confessions.

The Japanese police had kept Mark in jail since his initial arrest. Manseibashi police station officers said he had lost

15 kg in a few weeks. He was not allowed to have more than one visit a day, and was only allowed to read books in Japanese. Of course, he was not given access to a computer. The interrogation of Mark had some surreal moments. Interrogators asked him several times over several days if he was actually Satoshi Nakamoto. Mark did not confess to that either.

Yet among the many accusations pinned on Mark, including the improper transfer of electronic funds, the prosecution's statements never touched upon the 650,000 missing bitcoins (worth an estimated $390 million at the time).

At the end of October, the Japanese police arrested him on different embezzlement charges, accusing him of having used company funds to pay for his entertainment expenses and expenditures. He was accused of having moved 20 million yen ($166,000) in client money to his own bank. It seemed a piddling amount compared to everything that was at stake.

In fact, if Mark was spending his own money on prostitutes, it had nothing to do with the charges that were pending against him; of course, the implication was that he was using company money. Therefore, such salacious reporting was more than justified—at least for the newspapers and reporters stuck on the story.

He was arrested three times in total. Each arrest allowed the police and prosecutors to extend the roughly three weeks of incarceration allowed under Japanese law. During such interrogations, a lawyer is not allowed to be present.

Why did the police keep arresting Mark on separate charges, one after another? Because that's standard operating procedure. Ask Carlos Ghosn, once the chairman and CEO of Nissan, who had the bad luck of being betrayed by Japanese colleagues who wanted to see him out of power, and who the prosecutors thought would be an easy mark.

When the Japanese government wants to make a statement, foreign CEOs make great targets. And while the Japanese justice system theoretically operates on the principle of "innocent until proven guilty," in reality that's not quite the case.

This is how the criminal justice system works in Japan: If the police arrest you, you are expected to confess. When you don't comply, you keep getting arrested until you do confess. The longer you wait, the more charges they throw at you, the longer they can detain you, and the longer you can be interrogated. They expected Mark, a Japanophile, to behave like a proper suspect and to confess to the charges against him—even if he hadn't committed the crimes—so they could close the case.

The police and prosecutors will do anything to get a confession. The questions of guilt or innocence have very little to do with the Japanese justice system—it's more about winning and losing. And a confession is worth more than all the evidence in the world.

Here's an example. On November 24, 2015, the Tokyo High Court ruled that a fraud suspect, fifty-one years old, had been lured into a confession by police who had promised him a lighter sentence. He had been charged with multiple counts of fraud, allegedly because he had refused to confess to the initial charges. The defendant later retracted his confession and pleaded not guilty. His lawyer asked to cross-examine the police officers who had interrogated the subject, but the court rejected the request. The defendant was sentenced to five years in jail, and the sentence was appealed. The suspect then called the arresting officers, and recorded them admitting to having made a deal with him. On that basis, the Tokyo High Court, on appeal, ruled that the case had to be retried, and sent it back to the lower courts.

It was a rare moment in Japanese criminal justice. If the accused hadn't had the tape recording, he would have never been retried. And even then, he was still found guilty but given a reduced sentence.

You might ask yourself this: if Mark had 650,000 bitcoins stored away somewhere, why hadn't he run off to a desert island, like Roger Ver had? He could have been living it up in South America or somewhere else, with a new passport and a new life, instead of rotting in a Japanese holding cell. (Of course, in the long run, that didn't work out too well for Mr. Bitcoin Jesus, who, you may remember, was extradited to the US and fined heavily in 2024.) If Mark was guilty, why did he work so closely with the Japanese police and give them access to all his data? Why not erase the data before going bankrupt and get away with being charged with a relatively minor offense?

This strategy had worked brilliantly for the head of Japan's Incubator Bank several years before. The bank filed for bankruptcy in September 2010 at the Tokyo District Court after over-expanding and engaging in a number of allegedly illegal transactions, which resulted in it being shuttered. The collapse could have rocked the foundations of Japan's finance system, but the media downplayed it. It was the country's first bank failure in seven years, and was also the first case since the system's creation in 1971, when the government had limited its deposit guarantee to ¥10 million. Incubator Bank had net liabilities of ¥180.4 billion.

Takeshi Kimura, the chairman of the bank, and politically connected, ordered records to be destroyed as he got wind of Japan's Financial Services Agency getting ready to launch an investigation. He was found guilty of obstructing an inspection by the agency, and was given a suspended one-year prison term. In the end, he never even served time in jail. It was a case that proved if you're well connected and eliminate evidence, you may possibly get away with being charged for a much lesser crime: a mere slap on the wrist.

Mark could have tried a similar tactic. He could have easily wiped away almost all the transaction records and all the data in the servers, leaving little to investigate except for banking records. He didn't. He gave the data to cybercrime experts and the police, and attempted to figure out what had happened.

Maybe it was all a ruse. Maybe he was pretending to seek the real culprit to cover his own tracks.

The problem was that the Japanese justice system isn't really designed to uncover the truth—only to convict someone once they have been formally prosecuted.

Japan's criminal justice system has a stunning 99 percent conviction rate, which gives an ironic new meaning to the sobriquet "the 1 percent". Their success could be because their courts are just so wonderfully efficient. But that's not the case. Japan used to have a jury system. In 1943, the conviction rate was around 82 percent. After the war, the system was never revived, and the new system, in which professional judges determined the verdicts, made sure that the wheels of justice were ruthlessly efficient.

One of Japan's most noted defense attorneys, Hiroyuki Kawai, calls criminal cases in Japan "hostage trials." He explains that from the time you are arrested, including the forty-eight hours you may spend in police custody, you can be held for a total of twenty-three days—and you are not guaranteed the right to see a lawyer. Your lawyer may not be present during interrogation. Your lawyer might also fail to inform you of your only right, which is the right to remain silent.

Meanwhile, suspects routinely are interrogated for eight hours a day or more. It's a breeding ground for false confessions.

"The system is 'presumed innocent until proven guilty' in theory," says Kawai, "but the accused is routinely denied bail and held in confinement—unless they confess. If they don't confess, they're assumed to be in danger of destroying evidence that would convict them, which presumes that they're guilty in the first place. If they do confess, then later plead innocent, the judge doesn't believe the confession was coerced—thus they are almost sure to be found guilty." He notes that if a lawyer is unable to meet with their client, building a criminal defense is next to impossible.

The prosecutors in Japan hold all the cards. They do not have to show all the evidence in their possession to the defense. According to David Johnson, the author of *The Japanese Way of Justice*, there have been several cases in which prosecutors have concealed critical evidence that would have exonerated the accused, but such prosecutorial conduct is not considered a crime.

There has been at least one case of a prosecutor tampering with evidence to convict the accused. Another former prosecutor resigned from office, then wrote a book apologizing for browbeating innocent people into making false confessions, noting that he had been educated during his training to believe that "yakuza and foreigners have no human rights."

The Japanese police launched an investigation over a series of death threats made by a Japanese hacker starting in June 2012. The lone cyber malcontent posted the death threats on Japanese websites and sent out emails warning of terrorist attacks. This led to four false arrests and a major loss of face. At the end of June 2012, the police made their first arrest: a nineteen-year-old student attending Meiji University. He was accused of having posted death threats on the city of Yokohama's webpage.

In July, the true hacker posted on the Osaka City website, "I will commit a massacre in Osaka's streets. I will run over people, stab some at random and then kill myself." The post resulted in the arrest of the anime creative director Masaki Kitamura. Kitamura was indicted even while professing his innocence. By the end of September, the Tokyo, Osaka, Mie, and Fukuoka police departments had arrested two more people on charges of obstruction of business.

Seven months into the investigation, in February 2013, the police might have finally gotten their man.

A joint police task force, led by the Tokyo Metropolitan Police Department, arrested Yusuke Katayama, a thirty-year-old IT office worker, on charges of forcible obstruction of business. He had allegedly posted a threat on the online bulletin board 2-channel in August 2012. The threat stated that a mass murder would take place at a comic-book convention in Tokyo. It caused chaos and disrupted the event.

Katayama had allegedly used a computer virus to take over an innocent man's computer to post the threat. Katayama was suspected of having committed at least three other similar crimes. According to his lawyer, he denied the charges, but the FBI later presented evidence to the Japanese police that linked Katayama to a US server that had been used in the crimes. Nevertheless, with four mistaken arrests weighing on their shoulders, the Japanese police proceeded with due caution.

The arrest of Katayama ended one of Japan's strangest criminal cases in recent years—one that showed major flaws in the country's criminal justice system and its ability to investigate cybercrime. It was an investigation that gave a lone hacker national attention as he made fools out of Japan's law enforcement officers and challenged the police to catch him with a series of clues, taunts, false leads, and cryptic riddles. The police's success in answering his final puzzle, hidden in the collar of a cat on a Japanese island, may have proved to be his undoing.

Everything changed in October 2012, when emails claiming responsibility for the crimes were delivered first to Yoji Ochiai, a Tokyo lawyer, and then to the Tokyo Broadcasting System (TBS), as well as other media. The emails stated, "I am the real culprit," and were sent from a man using the name "Oni Koroshi," ("Demon Killer,") which is also the name of several different brands of sake in Japan, including a cheap version much beloved by the police, and sold in 100-yen (about $1) juice boxes in convenience stores, complete with plastic straws. Depending on where you are from in Japan, in rural areas, it's sometimes pronounced, "*Onigoroshi*" with a hard "g". Which led to some confusion when airing the story on Japanese television news, because the pronunciation varied.

Of course, because I drank cheap sake as a police reporter and because I'm a secret redneck, I preferred to call it Onigoroshi—but, as Shakespeare would say, it's still a terrible box of booze no matter what name you give it.

The emails from the demon killer contained details of how the crimes had been committed that only the criminal could have known. Koroshi discussed how he had spread a Trojan horse virus (in Japan, sometimes called a "remote-control virus") known as iesys.exe via online bulletin boards and had then remotely controlled the host computers to post the death threats.

In his email to the lawyer Ochiai, Koroshi stated that his goal was not to put innocent people in jail and to laugh about it. Instead, he wrote, "my motive is solely to entrap the police and prosecutors and expose their shameful status to the world." He insisted that he always intended to confess to the crimes in due time and to save the people who had been wrongly arrested. He said that he chose Ochiai because he had happened to see the lawyer on television and, he wrote, "you look like you understand these things."

The revelations in October began a game of cat-and-mouse between Oni Koroshi and the police. After the emails were made public, the police reopened their investigations, and by October 18 Yutaka Katagiri, the chief of Japan's National Police Agency (NPA), admitted that there might have been several false arrests made. On October 19, a joint investigation task force was set up to get to the bottom of the crime. By December, all four individuals who had been wrongfully arrested were cleared of all charges. On December

12, the NPA offered a reward of up to 3 million yen for information leading to an arrest.

According to NPA sources, the cybercrime squads in each police department had determined the IP addresses of the computers that were used to make the threats, but hadn't gone further to see if the computers had been affected by viruses or if they had had malicious software installed that would make them platforms for cybercrime, also known as "zombie computers." According to the *Mainichi* newspaper, none of the detectives investigating a death threat made in September even knew of the existence of remote-control viruses.

Oni Koroshi, aware of the police's inability to effectively conduct a cyber-investigation, taunted them in emails to the press, and even sent the police an email directly, saying, "Thank you for playing with me."

What made the slow investigation even more embarrassing for Japan's finest was that, in two cases, innocent people had been coerced into making false confessions. The reasons for their false confessions are still not entirely clear, but, as you already know, Japan has a 99 percent conviction rate for criminal cases that are indicted.

It's clear that the Japanese law enforcement made critical mistakes during the start of the investigation, thus stretching it out over half a year. However, it turns out the criminal also made some mistakes. The police were able to determine by November that one of the messages sent to the lawyer had gone through a US server, and they asked for the FBI's help in tracking the mail. According to the Japanese media, the task force dispatched investigators to the US on November 12, to speed up the information-sharing process.

Sources close to the investigation say the FBI found a copy of the virus in a US server that contained encoded information linking it to Katayama. There was also a careless mistake made in uploading the virus that allowed the route to be traced back to a computer that Katayama had had access to in Japan; this new evidence certainly didn't help Katayama's case. However, considering Oni Koroshi's ability to frame innocent people, nothing was conclusive.

It appears that after Japanese police were dispatched to the US, Koroshi started to get nervous and tried to cover his tracks. On November 13, 2012, he sent a message to the lawyer: "It's been a long time. I made a mistake. It looks like the game is over. It would be unpleasant to be caught so right now I'm going to commit suicide by hanging myself." The accompanying photo of a witch figurine with a computer cable, in the shape of a noose, wrapped around her got the attention of the police and the media. The tabloids were filled with speculation as to whether Oni Koroshi had really killed himself.

He didn't stay dead for very long.

On January 1, 2013, he sent a traditional Happy New Year's message to the Japanese media, encouraging them to go for a big scoop. On January 5, he sent the media new messages with a "puzzle for the coming spring" to solve. The task was to locate a cat on Enoshima Island, a popular tourist spot—a cat with a memory device in his collar that would yield clues about the criminal and his motives.

The police found a micro-SD card on a cat's collar the same day that the message was sent. In the chip was the source code for the virus, and buried in the source code was a message that said, "I was caught up in a crime and even though I was innocent, I had to drastically rearrange my life." Police sources said that a security camera on Enoshima had captured footage of a man resembling Katayama moving toward the cat. A further investigation of security cameras in the area revealed footage of a motorbike that allegedly belonged to Katayama, and this, along with other information, was used to get a warrant for his arrest. On background, an investigator said, "Due to the previous emails, we were looking for someone who had been convicted for similar crimes in the past. Katayama was already a person of interest by January."

The police also searched Katayama's home to look for evidence that he had sent the January 5 email. They seized ten computers from his home, and analyzed them. Several of the computers at the office where he worked were also found to have had the Tor software installed. Remember Tor? It's the network on which the dark web operates, and which was such an integral part of the Silk Road.

Police suspect that Katayama had used the PCs at his home or work to remotely access other computers and to send more than ten threats, either by posting them online or via email. It has also become apparent that if Katayama was Oni Koroshi, he certainly may have had motives for making fools out of the police: revenge. According to the *Mainichi Shimbun*, Katayama had been arrested in 2005 for posting death threats online and was convicted. The death threats pertained to what Katayama perceived as an insulting illustration of a cat, posted by a user on an internet bulletin board, who Katayama had never met. He was extremely unhappy with the sentence.

Katayama was reportedly a huge cat fan, and was a

frequent visitor to Tokyo's cat cafés, where customers can play with the cats that are kept as pets by the store owners. This, too, seems to link him to the code-carrying cat on Enoshima.

All that being said, for a while no one was sure that the Japanese police had finally nabbed the right man. Ochiai, the lawyer who had first been contacted by Oni Koroshi replied at the time to inquiries from the press as follows: "I can't help but feel a little uneasy. Is this really the criminal? Has there not been a mistake in identification? I hope the police diligently investigate. An arrest does not mean the real culprit has been caught. The police themselves have proven that point."

On February 4, 2015, the Tokyo District Court drew the curtain on the strange saga of Yusuke Katayama. He was sentenced to eight years of hard labor.

"A malicious cybercrime," presiding judge Katsunori Ono called it, noting how Katayama had twisted the lives of the innocent, setting traps that caught others in a net meant for himself. Four people, including a former minor, had been wrongfully hauled in on suspicion, their lives upended by Katayama's digital puppetry.

Judge Ono, not one to sugarcoat his findings, laid out the motives: a mix of ego and a simmering grudge against authority. It was a game to Katayama, a test of wits against the state, a way to show he was cleverer than the system that had been trying to catch him. But the court wasn't in the business of rewarding cleverness when it left collateral damage in its wake. "There is no aspect of the defendant's self-centered motives that warrants sympathy," Ono stated, his tone leaving no room for ambiguity.

The wrongful arrests, not formally part of the charges, but very much the fallout of Katayama's twisted play, added weight to the gavel's descent.

Remember, Katayama had first been arrested in February 2013, denying all charges with the sort of wide-eyed sincerity that plays well on the evening news. He claimed he had been framed, a hapless victim of a hacker more skilled than himself. But in May 2014, out on bail and perhaps bored with waiting to see which way the wind would blow, he had sent emails to the media, purportedly being from the real criminal. When those same emails were traced back to him, he made a full confession

Judge Ono didn't flinch in characterizing the act. "An unprecedented and egregious attempt at cover-up," he said—the kind of remark that lands with the thud of finality. But the judge didn't have much to say that was critical of the police—who had arrested the wrong people and had browbeaten at least two of them into confessing to crimes they hadn't committed.

What the lawyer Ochiai said remains true: "An arrest does not mean the real culprit has been caught. The police themselves have proven that point."

Those are words to live by. The Japanese prosecutors don't seem to give them much credence. The prosecutors in Japan only pick slam-dunk cases; if they can't win, they don't take the case to court.

As we've seen, the police and prosecutors do everything possible to obtain a confession, and the best way to achieve that is to keep the accused a prisoner. The police had rearrested Mark Karpelès twice to keep him in jail for as long as possible, hoping for a confession. They were even hoping for a fourth arrest, but were deterred by an official in the Ministry of Justice who said that it was an abuse of the system to keep arresting one man on similar charges again and again. The prosecutors ended up filing an indictment with secondary charges so that, if they failed to convict him on the main charges, they might get lucky with the other charges. At one point in the back and forth between the prosecutors and the defense, the judge became quite angry with the prosecutors, referencing a Japanese proverb while scolding them: "'If you shoot enough bullets, you'll hit something' doesn't apply to the criminal law. Get your shit together." (*"Ii kagen ni shiro."*)

There are several ways you could translate the last sentence said to the prosecutors at that moment, and none of them sound judge-like, but let me assure you that "Get your shit together" is probably the closest equivalent.

They stopped rearresting Mark, but he wasn't going to get out of jail yet—not for a very long time.

CHAPTER TEN

What really happened

Mark was released on bail on July 14, 2016, almost a year after his arrest. He looked like a ghost of himself. It was clear that it hadn't been easy on him: the food had been awful; the stress, immense. A young woman who had been detained at the Harajuku holdings cell for twenty-one days called it "the detention diet—you're guaranteed to lose weight."

He was thin, pale, and trembling. Clad in his *Tokyo Ghoul* T-shirt, he appeared gaunter than ever—like a teenager who had borrowed his father's clothes. Nathalie and I took him out for coffee and cinnamon toast at our favorite café in Shimo-Kitazawa, the same place where I had warned him not to confess to the police. The old Mark would have inhaled the cinnamon toast. He nibbled at the food, but he seemed to have no appetite. He did show a spark of the old foodie Mark when remarking on how good the caramelized glaze was on the thick buttery toast. We asked him what he wanted to do now.

He said, "I want to find out who really stole the bitcoins and how they did it. I want to clear my name."

Fortunately for Mark, while he had been in jail, Kim Nilsson, Nathalie, and I had been working on solving that very problem. While Kim had been working his magic on the blockchain analysis, Nathalie and I were still following the Bitcoin story and were in constant touch with Mark and his lawyer.

Mark told us that, at one time prior to his arrest, he had been approached by US government officials about his case. This struck us as odd. I also had a talk with a federal law enforcement officer about the Mt. Gox case that I couldn't make sense of, and was intrigued. With Mark's permission, Nathalie searched his desk for the business cards of the federal agents he'd spoken with. The results were surprising.

When you spread them out on the desk, they represented a strange cast of characters. John R. Davidson, the assistant legal attaché at the embassy from the FBI, was someone I already knew: he was a good guy, but tight-lipped. However, among the other business cards was one for Kathryn Haun, from the DOJ's United States Attorney's Office in San Francisco. There was a business card for Yuki Tsuchiya, an inspector at the Cyber Crime Division of the National Police Agency; a card for Katsuhiko Inoue, the chief inspector of the International Investigative Operations Division (Interpol Tokyo)—who was a member of the National Police Agency and an Interpol liaison; and a card for a special investigator from the criminal investigative division of the Internal Revenue Service (IRS). Ironically, one of the business cards also belonged to the police officer who had come to arrest Mark on that day long ago on August 1, 2015.

What the fuck was going on?

At first, we thought it might have to do with the Silk Road investigation—but that wasn't it at all. After googling Haun's name, we found that she had been one of the prosecutors in charge of the Carl Mark Force IV and Shaun Bridges investigation; she'd been instrumental in the successful outcome of the case. In July 2015, as mentioned in chapter eight, Force had admitted to everything. He pleaded guilty to charges of money laundering, obstruction of justice, and extortion under color of official right—a fancy way to say egregious abuse of his Secret Service status. He was sentenced to seventy-eight months in prison. Bridges also pleaded guilty to money laundering and obstruction of justice, and was given seventy-one months in prison; later, he was found guilty of stealing even more bitcoins than previously thought. The judge tacked another two years onto his sentence.

The IRS agent's name led us in a different direction. We realized that the agency propelling the investigation into these corrupt cops was the IRS—not the FBI, and not the Secret Service. We tried to get an on-the-record interview with a colleague of the special agent in charge, but with no luck. We, of course, reached out to IRS Special Agent Tigran Gambaryan, the man whose name was on the business card, and who, because of his incredibly ground-breaking analysis of the blockchain and bitcoin transactions, was known in the cyberworld as "The Blockchain Wizard." His affidavit in the Silk Road Dirty Cop case read like a superbly researched docudrama, and his explanation of Bitcoin was masterful. It was so good that we borrowed it for this book.

We became instant Tigran fans as well. Trust me when I tell you that there aren't many special agents in the IRS who have fans on the internet. Tigran does, because he's a great detective.

Mark wasn't sure what the government officials wanted from him, or what they wanted to talk to him about. He suspected it had something to do with the Silk Road investigation, but he didn't know any more than that. Meanwhile, Kim was reaching some conclusions about the identity of the hacker. We were talking to Kim, but he became increasingly vague in his answers. One thing I noticed was that his tone had changed. He didn't seem to regard Mark as the culprit in the Bitcoin heist anymore. It was a subtle thing, but picking up verbal and nonverbal clues is part of my job. We would also have coffee with Kim on a regular basis, but it wasn't helping us much. He knew more than we did.

Now, if you've been a reporter in Japan long enough, a stack of business cards is a good lead. It's actually a great lead. After I followed this up—and took a trip to New York to do it—it seemed to me that US government agents were engaging in another investigation completely unrelated to Silk Road or the corrupt investigators. They were looking for a thief or a ring of thieves involved in Bitcoin heists worldwide.

That raised two possibilities:

(1) They wanted to talk to Mark because the criminal had used Mt. Gox to launder money, and gaining access to the Mt. Gox records would help them capture or identify the criminal.

(2) Not only did they want Mark's help in identifying and capturing the criminal, but Mt. Gox had also been

hacked by the same group or individual.

If the latter explanation was true, it would mean that Mark was innocent. At this time, though, neither Nathalie nor I thought that was very likely. Stucky kept plugging away, and she got word that US special agents were coming to Japan to talk to Japanese police. It was all vague. The US was apparently running an investigation into an international Bitcoin heist involving something called "WME," and they were seeking cooperation with their investigation.

I had no idea what WME meant. Was it an acronym? A code-name?

We managed to contact one of the special agents who'd come to meet the Japanese police. We asked for a meeting, thinking it was a waste of time. However, not only did they agree to meet with us, but they wanted to talk to us. In fact, they were looking forward to speaking with us—on one condition. We were told: "This is an informal meeting. Anything official has to go through our headquarters in DC and the embassy."

This was amazing to us. Years before, when investigating a deal that the FBI had made with a Japanese gangster, I can't say that anyone from the agency involved was happy to talk about it with me. It was like pulling teeth. It took a tremendous amount of stealth, bluffing, bullying, and appealing to their sense of justice to get a few agents to confirm my findings.

And yet now we had a special agent working on an international case of Bitcoin hacking who actually wanted to meet us—and talk to us. It would be on background, but the agent was going to meet us.

Personally, when it came to Bitcoin, I always felt that

Nathalie and I were the reverse of special agents Dana Scully and Fox Mulder from the classic paranormal investigation series *The X Files*.

She was more like Agent Mulder, who believes in UFOs and aliens. She wanted to believe that Bitcoin was a viable and important cryptocurrency. She believed that the real criminal wasn't Mark. That there was a conspiracy to get him convicted. That the truth was out there.

I didn't think so. I was like the skeptical agent, Dr. Scully. I thought Bitcoin was a crazy idea. I thought that the truth was obvious. Mark had lost the bitcoins or stolen them himself, and there was no real culprit out there. The only person to blame was Mark.

On the day before the envoy arrived, I met Nathalie at Krispy Kreme Donuts near Yurakucho station. My son, Ray, was visiting for the summer, so I took him with me. He understood the concept of Bitcoin, so I knew he wouldn't be bored. Over coffee and green tea-flavored donuts, we discussed what we would ask at the meeting and what we already knew.

Our contact got in late. It was none other than Tigran Gambaryan. The special agent whose business card we had found on Mark's desk. The guy who had refused to answer our emails. Over the phone, we suggested meeting at a Japanese pub over drinks and yakitori. Tigran was up for that, and we managed to get a private room: tatami, a low table, and some quiet. And so, one summer night, Nathalie, Tigran, and I got drunk together and talked about Bitcoin, Carl Force IV, Mt. Gox, and Mark Karpelès.

Tigran, originally an Armenian immigrant, hadn't turned up in a suit: he wore a black T-shirt and jeans. With his bulging biceps, he looked like someone who spent a lot of time in the gym, and he had a neatly trimmed beard and an easy-going manner. He was jovial, and spoke with a deep, rolling voice. In some ways, he seemed more like the smartest auto-mechanic in the garage than he did a special agent or "the block-chain wizard." He was surprisingly likeable.

It was a very long night. Nathalie played the perfect hostess, pouring drinks regularly, and asking open questions that generated long answers. She was much more charming than I was, and she understood Bitcoin much better.

Halfway through the evening, I realized something important. What the FBI, the IRS, the DOJ, and HSI were all trying to do was catch the person who had really stolen the bitcoins from Mt. Gox. Not only had this individual or group of thieves raided Mt. Gox, but they had also apparently been behind the robbery of *Bitcoinica* and other cryptocurrency exchanges.

I was kind of excited—but I didn't want to appear completely in the dark. So I asked simply, "If you were doing the Karpelès case in the US, what would you nab him for?"

Tigran's answer was instantaneous: "Nothing really. Possibly breach of trust. But he didn't break any laws. He's just a shitty business manager. He should have known those bitcoins were gone long before he did. But he's a victim, not a villain."

I almost choked on my hot sake.

"When were they stolen?"

"I'm guessing between 2011—the first big heist—and then gradually siphoned off until somewhere in the middle of

2013, but I don't know. That's why I'm here. I need the Mt. Gox database so I can figure it all out."

"Why don't you ask the Japanese police for it," I asked him.

"I have. They won't cooperate. That's why I'm asking you. What the fuck? You understand the police. Why am I getting stonewalled?"

I tried to give the police the benefit of the doubt—maybe they didn't have the whole database. Maybe they were concerned about the chain of evidence. But then I told him what I really thought.

"They won't give you the database because they don't want you to catch the person or persons that actually hacked into Mt. Gox and stole the 650,000 bitcoins. It will make them look like idiots. It doesn't help their case at all. Or, as the Japanese say, *hyakugai ari, ichiri nashi*—one hundred damages, and not one bit of profit."

"That's shitty."

"Yes, it is," I concurred.

"What's wrong with them? I mean, what are they hoping to prove?"

"The prosecutors hate to lose. Cops hate to lose face. They're already worried about getting a guilty verdict with the charges they've indicted him for. The revelation that the Japanese police didn't catch the real thief makes them look incompetent. It also makes it obvious that Mark was arrested on weak charges to force a confession to a crime he didn't actually commit. Helping you could prove something that undermines the whole reason for the investigation in the first place."

"What do you mean?"

And so, for the benefit of Tigran, I explained what I have just explained to you about Japan's legal system, until Tigran was nodding.

"So, you're saying that, because the entire reason there was an investigation into the collapse of Mt. Gox and Mark Karpelès in the first place was because of the theft of the 650,000 bitcoins, if it was actually someone else that did it, the whole *raison d'être* of the investigation is called into doubt?"

"Exactly. I'm not sure what *raison d'être* actually means, because my French is nonexistent, but if someone else hacked Mt. Gox, it begs the question: Why is Mark in jail, and why the hell didn't the Japanese police catch the real criminal? It makes them look as stupid as they looked in the cat case."

"Wow."

After we had a cigarette break, Nathalie got straight to the point.

"So, you mean if you had the database, you could prove that someone else hacked Mt. Gox, not Mark?"

Tigran hesitated.

"I don't know. I don't know if all the coins that went missing were stolen. But I think that a substantial amount of them, or even the majority of them, might have been stolen by this entity we are looking for. And if we had complete access to the Mt. Gox database, we could identify this person and track them down."

"Person?"

"Entity."

"Individual?"

"Entity."

I took that exchange to mean they had narrowed it down to one person. I nodded as he doubled down on being vague. As we continued to talk, I had an idea.

"If we can get you the database, would you promise to make it clear that the criminal also hacked Mt. Gox along with the other exchanges?"

Tigran scrunched up his face and took a deep breath. We waited for an answer.

"If you get us the database for Mt. Gox, the whole thing, and we catch the guy—yes, I will make sure that it's very clear."

I pushed harder. "By clear, this means you'll put out a press release?"

Tigran sighed.

"Okay. If you hold up your end of the bargain."

I felt like I was on a roll, so I pushed again.

"And can we get a twenty-four-hour heads-up before the arrest, or be first in line for the release after the arrest?"

The response was immediate.

"No fucking way. Definitely not before the arrest, but I could see you got notice after the arrest—if there is ever an arrest. Which there may not be."

So we had a deal.

The deal relied on trust—on both sides—and it relied on getting Mark to give us a copy of the database.

He was still in jail.

If he had the database. There was also one other problem that occurred to me as we left the table in a collectively good mood.

The Mt. Gox database of transactions, some of which had been partially leaked, would take up terabytes of data.

It would be more data than could possibly be sent over the internet in any reasonable fashion. This meant that unless I could get the database to Tigran within forty-eight hours, while he was still in Japan, one of us would have to carry the hard drive to the United States and hand it over to the investigators.

Later that night, Stucky and I messaged each other back and forth about the meeting. She had set it up: without her, there would have been no meeting. We would have been kept in the dark.

And then it dawned on me why they had met us with. It was like the flash of satori that I had always hoped to have as a student of Zen Buddhism.

They needed our help.

I wrote:

It was very good to meet him. Thank you. Be sure to thank Tigran.

We learned an important thing from that meeting.

I believe Mark is just sloppy. It's not a crime.

Every instinct I have tells me he's (Mark) telling you and me the truth. I gotta get some sleep. I'll call in the afternoon or morning.

This was the most important meeting we had.

She wrote back: "Understood. Yes, I don't want to trick no one. I'll write Tigran."

We still didn't know who WME was. And neither did the US government. They thought he might be Bulgarian. They knew he was connected to a cryptocurrency exchange called BTC-e that had sprung into existence right around the time that Mt. Gox had been first hacked in a major way.

Mark agreed to provide the data. It turned out that he had preemptively prepared the hard disk a week before his arrest, just in case he couldn't be released. For someone who advertised that they were "Effortless French", he made great efforts to stay ahead of the curve. He had kept a copy, locked up and encrypted. We were told where to pick it up.

Roughly a month later, I went to California with all the data inside a small portable hard drive. We could have mailed it to the investigators, but that seemed too risky.

I found the cheapest flight I could, and paid for it out of my own pocket. I reasoned to myself that $600 was worth it if it set an innocent man free. And I had friends in San Francisco. So why not?

Setting up the hand-off was no easy thing. There was a chain of evidence that needed to be followed, and my emails kept getting longer as we hashed out the details.

Most of the time, I dealt with Tigran. I wrote to him in late August:

> I understand that discretion is warranted, and I understand that your investigation is separate from those of the Japanese authorities. I have no desire to put you guys in a tight place. I would ask that, as a general courtesy, you simply consider that Mark Karpelès is cooperating not purely out of self-interest and that he's had his name leaked to the wrong people before. So convincing him to do this wasn't easy. Please tell me who to hand it over to. I'd like to make sure I hand it to someone who will take good care of it.

He wrote me back on August 23:

> I spoke with the prosecutors I am working with (CCed). You can drop it off at the U.S. Attorney's office in SF. Just so we are clear, we can't make any promises. We will look at the data and make a determination based on the evidence. No PGP, but you can use Veracrypt.

By the time I was ready to go to the US to meet an agent in person, Immigrations Customs Enforcement, the Department of Justice, the IRS, the FBI, the District Attorney, the Secret Service, and agencies I'd never even heard of were in the email chain.

But when I arrived in San Francisco on September 2, there was a big problem. I was supposed to hand over the materials at:

> 450 Golden Gate Avenue. It's a federal building. [Your contact] may be on the 9th floor, but they occupy additional floors in the building, which is why I say that he will give you the details for his office. The building has strong security, which requires you to have proper/valid ID to enter. If you have any issues, please call me at my cell.

The problem: it was Labor Day Weekend. And the agent who was supposed to pick up the disk wasn't available. Monday, September 5 was Labor Day, and I didn't have a ticket that would let me stick around that long.

So a frantic email chain began until someone was located who could take the drive from me. And they needed to be a Special Agent, so that the chain of evidence wasn't broken.

In a federal investigation, "the chain of evidence" is more than just a bureaucratic term—it's the spine of the case, the unbroken line that connects a piece of evidence from the scene of the crime to the courtroom. It's the proof that what was found, tested, and analyzed is the same item being shown to the jury, untouched by dirty hands or careless mistakes. Each step in this chain needs to be logged with almost obsessive precision: who collected it, who handled it, when it changed hands, and under what conditions it was kept. One weak link, one missed signature or unexplained gap, and the defense pounces: the evidence, no matter how damning, risks being tossed as tainted.

In the world of investigations, integrity isn't just a concept; it's a ledger with every name, date, and detail accounted for. In other words, federal investigations are supposed to have their own sort of blockchain.

After phone calls and a chain of emails that basically told me everyone who was working the investigation, I found someone who could meet up with me.

Finally, I was able to hand over the hard drive in a seedy bar close to a federal building to Bryan Wong, a Special Agent with the IRS.[*] He took it out of my hands and bought me a drink for my troubles. I ordered a Malibu Coke, just to be cheeky. I took a day to relax before flying back to Japan. There were some follow-up emails, and then mostly radio silence. We were told that the database had been useful.

While back in Japan, Nathalie and I continued to gather information until we were pretty sure we knew exactly who "WME" really was, and that he was probably Russian. In fact, we had prepared a 110-page article about the case that was

---

[*] Brian Wong passed away a few years ago. Rest in peace. He was a highly respected Special Agent.

being edited for publication in the summer of 2017. Nathalie and I had a fierce argument over whether we could put the name "WME" in the manuscript, or how specific we could be regarding nationality. I wanted to say Russian, which was way too specific. Nathalie argued for "Eurasian," which seemed overly broad. I suggested "a hacker from the former Soviet Union," which was true: Russia was part of the Soviet Union. Then everything went up in smoke when I got a cryptic phone call and a link to a Department of Justice press release that hadn't yet been posted. WME had been caught.

We raced to get the story to *The Daily Beast*. This was the culmination of everything we had been working on:

The World's Most Infamous Billion-Dollar Bitcoin Launderer Nabbed at Last?

The Russian known as WME has links to computer hacking, ransomware scams, identity theft, tax refund fraud schemes, corrupt politicians, and drug trafficking around the world.

Homeland Security Investigations, The Internal Revenue Service—Criminal Investigation Division, and other federal agencies, working together with Greek police, have arrested the alleged mastermind behind a $4 billion money laundering scheme that used bitcoin transactions.

He is also believed to have played a role in the looting of Mt. Gox, once the world's largest bitcoin exchange, which went bankrupt in February 2014. The CEO, Mark Karpelès, is currently on trial for embezzlement and other charges in Japan.

The US Department of Justice identified the so-called

mastermind as Russian national Alexander Vinnik, aged thirty-eight. He was arrested in Greece, on a US warrant, with a wide array of electronic equipment that was confiscated.

The police said that Vinnik was involved in the management of "one of the largest cyber-crime websites in the world. (BTC-e)."

Vinnik has been accused of laundering billions of dollars since 2011 using bitcoin. The virtual currency was created by the mysterious Satoshi Nakamoto, is difficult to trace, and has reached values of up to $3,000 for a single bitcoin in recent months.

Because of the anonymity involved in bitcoin transactions, it became the currency of choice for the world's largest underground cyber market, Silk Road, where drugs, guns, and other forbidden goods were freely sold. American agents investigating Silk Road were also arrested for pilfering bitcoins while working the case and one was sentenced to six years for his malfeasance.

Vinnik is wanted in the US and could be extradited to face charges and a subsequent trial. He is allegedly a key figure in solving a number of bitcoin exchange hackings that have taken place in the last several years.

US law enforcement sources have long believed Vinnik was the real identity of "WME"—an almost legendary figure one federal agent called "the Keyser Söze of bitcoin money laundering," referring to the mysterious master criminal in the 1995 movie "The Usual Suspects." WME is believed to have played a role in the liquidation of bitcoins stolen from exchanges such as Bitcoinica and Bitfloor. Allegedly under the moniker WME, he complained about coins being confiscated from his accounts and also sold "discounted bitcoins" in net forums and on the dark web.

Police sources also confirmed that Vinnik played a role in the disappearance of 650,000 bitcoins hacked from Mt. Gox, once the world's largest bitcoin exchange between 2012 and 2014.

Mark had been more or less exonerated. The mystery had been solved, and it had taken years for it to happen. Immediately after the arrest, Kim Nilsson came forward and explained his role in the investigation.

Although everyone thought that bitcoin transactions were anonymous and that individuals couldn't be identified, Kim and Tigran Gambaryan *had* proved them wrong. The blockchain, the public ledger of Bitcoin, is maintained by thousands of computers all over the world. Transactions on it are public knowledge and can be seen by anyone, but the users making those transactions are theoretically invisible. However, because most bitcoin transactions are done through currency exchanges, like Mt. Gox or Bitcoinica, it is possible to identify individuals or entities. It is also possible to track bitcoins themselves.

While the blockchain is a revolutionary idea, Mt. Gox was basically a traditional financial institution, one that holds the currency of its customers in online accounts while connecting buyers with sellers. That was the problem.

Vinnik allegedly had hacked into the website and gained access to the private accounts of Mt. Gox in 2011, and began to steal bitcoins from the firm's online wallets (hot wallets), continuing to steal until 2013, until eventually stealing 630,000 bitcoins or more in a four-year period. Because Mark never reconciled the accounts, he didn't realize how much he had lost while money was coming in. (An additional 20,000 bitcoins were lost in spill-off from the hacking and problems with Mt. Gox's system.)

Kim Nilsson, by creating a program to index the blockchain and, later, by partnering with Mark, was able to trace the stolen bitcoins to an account owned by the individual known as WME at BTC-e, a dubious cryptocurrency exchange. And when Nilsson started looking at all the coins flowing into WME's account, he noticed that other stolen bitcoins were ending up with WME as well.

In April 2015, he published his findings on a blog, and, without tipping his hat, he sketched out what he knew and stated his belief that Mark had not stolen the bitcoins.

The blog post was noticed by someone important. You may remember the name: Gary Alford. Alford was the IRS special agent who had identified Ross Ulbricht as the founder of Silk Road. He contacted Kim and asked for his help.

Eventually, in the summer of 2016, through a mixture of cyber-sleuthing and good old-fashioned googling, Kim Nilsson was able to identify WME as none other than Alexander Vinnik. It was the same summer that we had had our fateful sit-down with agents working the case.

Kim sent the name to Gary Alford. The rest is history.

Gambaryan, who was the lead agent on the Vinnik case, told me that early on in the investigation, "No one knew who BTC-e was. No one knew who the owners were, but we knew that BTC-e would accept money from anyone and that they had no problems laundering stolen bitcoin."

Because Russia rarely extradites cybercriminals, the US waited for their chance to arrest Vinnik when they knew he'd be on holiday. On July 25, in Greece, undercover officers arrested him on the beach, in the shadows of an ancient monastery. They seized from him two tablet computers, two laptops, five cell-phones, and one router. He waited in a Greek jail, facing charges in the US, Russia, and France of hacking, computer fraud, money laundering, and other offenses.

Despite being the world's first real "bitcoin private investigator," Kim Nilsson was never paid for his work. He hasn't even recovered the twelve bitcoins he lost in the collapse of Mt. Gox.

"The real irony of all this is that what brought down Vinnik was in fact Mt. Gox and Mark Karpelès. Mark Karpelès had put into place security measures to avoid laundering stolen bitcoins, and that resulted in some of Vinnik's stolen loot being confiscated. Vinnik had an online temper tantrum about it, and stupidly used his real name. That's how he got caught," Kim explained to us.

So how did it all go down?

Well, Vinnik didn't do it alone.

We now know, according to some unsealed indictments, an announcement from the Department of Justice, and intelligence from agents who worked the case, what really happened.

There was this announcement from the Department of Justice:

Friday, June 9, 2023
The U.S. The Attorney's Office, Northern District of California and The Department of Justice today unsealed charges related to the 2011 hack of the cryptocurrency

exchange Mt. Gox and the operation of the illicit cryptocurrency exchange BTC-e. Alexey Bilyuchenko, 43, and Aleksandr Verner, 29, both Russian nationals, are charged with laundering approximately 647,000 bitcoins from their hack of Mt. Gox. Bilyuchenko was also charged with conspiring with Alexander Vinnik to operate BTC-e from 2011 to 2017.

However, you could read the full press release, all the court documents, and it would still be hard to follow. So allow me to break it down for you.

It all started in 2011 when a couple of Russian gentlemen, Alexey Bilyuchenko and Aleksandr Verner, decided to dip their hands into the virtual cookie jar that was Mt. Gox, then the world's largest Bitcoin exchange. It was a cookie jar filled with digital gold. They didn't break the cookie jar or pry it open; instead, they used a little cyber grease to quietly take the lid off the jar, stole a bunch of digital gold cookies, and put the lid back on. They'd wait—and then do it again.

The Mt. Gox hack wasn't about brute force—it was about finding the weakest link in a duct-taped system. Early in 2011, the pair exploited vulnerabilities in Mt. Gox's security, specifically targeting the server holding the private keys for customer wallets. Think of private keys as the PIN codes to a bank vault, and Mt. Gox, apparently, left the vault door slightly ajar.

Using their unauthorized access, the hackers manipulated the exchange's system to transfer bitcoins from Mt. Gox's wallets into their own. This wasn't a smash-and-grab; they worked patiently and methodically, draining funds bit by bit over three years. Essentially, they turned the world's largest

Bitcoin exchange into their personal ATM.

Using a bit of technical know-how and, presumably, the moral compass of a Bond villain, the three criminals eventually walked away with 647,000 bitcoins. They transferred the stolen money to addresses they controlled, quietly bleeding Mt. Gox dry while the exchange kept operating like a zombie, seemingly unaware it was hemorrhaging customer funds.

Investigators say that Bilyuchenko knew that he couldn't launder the money alone. So he reached out to Alexander Vinnik to do it. Vinnik'S BTC-e was a no-questions-asked crypto exchange for cybercriminals. In case you've forgotten, BTC-e wasn't just a cryptocurrency money-laundering operation; it was the biggest and baddest money-laundering operation, helping hackers, ransomware gangs, and assorted shady characters clean their stolen loot for a modest fee.

But stealing the bitcoins was just step one. The real magic was in laundering it. They funneled the coins through other exchanges and even a fraudulent "advertising contract" with a New York broker. This was all designed to conceal the origins of the loot. It was a classic con with a crypto twist: hide the stolen goods in plain sight, spread them across the globe, and hope no one notices. Spoiler alert: they noticed.

Eventually, the long arm of the law—represented here by the FBI, the IRS, the Secret Service, the Blockchain Wizard (Tigran), and a cast of hundreds—caught up with them. The DOJ made the arrests and unsealed the indictments, and the message was clear: even if your crimes are digital and your servers are buried in the bowels of the dark net, you're not beyond reach.

The precise how of the hack remains murky in detail, but the indictment suggests it involved a mix of server exploitation, poor internal security practices, and Mt. Gox's blissful ignorance.

Former Special Agent Tigran Gambaryan sums it up like this: "They [Vinnik and company] essentially took over the wallets and slowly drained the funds because Mark wasn't checking his cold storage."

By the time the exchange realized that something was wrong, the hackers had already emptied the vault and left the building. Turns out, the only thing worse than trusting your money to an unregulated crypto exchange is trusting one that treats cybersecurity like an afterthought—especially one where the motto of the CEO is "Should be fine."

Nowadays, when I want to tell my co-workers to expect disaster, I just turn to them, smile, and say, "Should be fine."

They know exactly what that means.

Perhaps we should give Mark Karpelès the final word about the investigation. He once told us, "I have seen things that others will never see." We know now that he was referring to the relative unlikelihood of the real criminal ever being caught. At least we can all see the truth now.

Mark posted these thoughts on the day that Vinnik's arrest was announced:

> Considering the efforts that went into this investigation and were required to reach this point, I dare say that there was little chance for us at MtGox to detect this at the time, especially considering the fact we were already fighting on various fronts, from compliance to daily hacking attempts to various other issues. At the time of my arrest the Japanese

police was still convinced there was no theft of Bitcoins at all from MtGox. Only few people suspected there could be an actual theft at the time, and my arrest was seen for a bit at the final point of the MtGox saga.

And yet, here we are. I must say this is something I have been waiting for this since that day of February 2014 when I stood in front of the cameras to announce the bankruptcy of MtGox. As far as I am concerned the Mt. Gox thief has been finally arrested. He stole some 630,000 BTC from MtGox (according to WizSec [Kim Nilsson]), but he also stole much more from everyone involved.

Russia, France, and the United States fought over who would get to extradite Vinnik first, and in 2019 (after a three-month-long hunger strike by Vinnik the year before) a judge finally made the decision. France would get him first, then the United States would have their turn, and then finally Vinnik would be allowed to be extradited back home to Russia. France put him behind bars in 2020. In May 2024, facing the end of his sentence in a French prison, Vinnik pleaded guilty to conspiracy to commit money laundering in the United States, facing up to twenty years in an American prison. His co-conspirators were still caught in the American justice system but they were not going to walk away. Justice would finally be served ... or so it would seem.

It would be so nice if we could end the book this way. But, unfortunately, justice is something very hard to find in this world. Even with a fistful of Bitcoin.

Epilogue

When I first drafted this epilogue (for the French version) on Christmas night 2018, it was all about price predictions and criminal convictions. Bitcoin was hovering at a value of just above $3,000, Japanese economists were promising no more roller-coaster rides, and Mark Karpelès was facing ten years in prison. Noted Japanese economist Yukio Noguchi assured us we'd never see Bitcoin touch $20,000 again. He'd be quite embarrassed now, I imagine, because in 2021 Bitcoin didn't just touch $20,000—it catapulted to over $60,000. So much for "never." Economists should never underestimate the power of collective delusions.

Now it's 2025, and we live in a world where the value of a single Bitcoin is dancing around $100,000. The lure of cryptocurrency is so powerful that even the world's greatest shyster and conman, Donald J. Trump, has gotten into the business. Trump's foray into cryptocurrency was as inevitable as it was audacious—a gilded hustle wrapped in patriotic pageantry and thinly veiled opportunism. Marketed as "World Liberty Financial," the platform launched on September 16, 2024, promising a financial revolution as defiant as its namesake, one that would liberate the faithful from the clutches of conventional finance. It will probably only liberate fiat currency out of the pockets of the suckers who trust him, and find its way into his bank accounts. But then again, who knows?

On November 5, 2024, Donald Trump was re-elected as the president of the United States. The world seemed to have realized that he was now looking to cryptocurrency as his latest conflict-of-interest grift, and would loosen regulations governing it. On November 10, the news propelled the price of a single bitcoin to $80,000 for the first time ever. Other cryptocurrencies saw their value increase by 9 percent.

The Financial Times quoted finance professor David Yermack, who threw some cold water on the boom. "Trump has made some wild promises on the campaign trail. But when you listen to him actually talk about digital currency, he has no idea what it is."

Among Trump's campaign promises was one surprise particularly pertinent to this book. On January 21, 2025, President Trump—who never met a grifter he didn't admire—granted a "full and unconditional" pardon to the man once known as Dread Pirate Roberts and the mastermind behind Silk Road: Ross Ulbricht.

The president called Ulbricht's mother to deliver the good news, which was a touching little Hallmark moment—if you ignore the part where her son had run a digital speakeasy for fentanyl and AK-47s. Or that he had allegedly tried to kill several people.

Ross Ulbricht was supposed to die in prison. Two life sentences plus forty years is arithmetic overkill, meant to send a message. The message, of course, being: Don't build a billion-dollar online drug empire unless you work for a Fortune 500 pharmaceutical company.

Trump, as always, didn't miss the opportunity to settle some scores. He took to his personal playground, Truth Social, and railed against "the scum" who had convicted Ulbricht, claiming they were the same "lunatics" persecuting him.

Predictably, libertarians lost their minds with joy. They had been advocating for Ulbricht's release for years, viewing his life sentence without parole as a stark example of government overreach in the war on drugs and online commerce. When the party extended an invitation to Donald Trump to speak at their national convention in May 2024, he had seized the opportunity to court their support. Trump's appearance at the convention was met with a mix of hostility and enthusiasm. His speech was frequently interrupted by jeers and boos from attendees skeptical of his commitment to libertarian principles, but the mood shifted when he addressed Ulbricht's case. As soon as he promised clemency, a significant portion of the crowd erupted in cheers.

"If you vote for me, on day one, I will commute the sentence of Ross Ulbricht," Trump declared, a statement that instantly became one of the most talked-about moments of his speech. Trump basked in their applause, feeding off it like a vampire at a blood drive.

So it happened that in late January 2025, Ulbricht, freshly released from a federal prison in Arizona, was officially a free man. His lawyer, Joshua Dratel, called it a victory for justice, while prosecutors who had once warned of the lasting damage of Silk Road were left wondering if their profession was still a thing. After his release, Ulbrich took to X (formerly Twitter) with a video. Looking clean cut and boyish, and adopting a slow, peaceful air, he said:

> I am so, so grateful to have my life back, to have my future back, to have this second chance. This is such an important moment for me and for my whole family, and it's an important moment for everybody who's been working for this for years. This is a victory and it's your victory, too. And this is an important moment for everybody, everywhere, who loves freedom, and who cares about second chances.

I called Tigran Gambaryan the day after Ulbrich's release, when he expressed his mixed feelings:

> Having been involved in the Silk Road corruption investigation, I spent countless hours reviewing conversations between Ross and various individuals. I find myself conflicted about this development. On one hand, the evidence shows Ross arranged for the murder of several individuals—plans that, while ultimately not carried out, were very real in his mind. On the other hand, I recognize that Ross was a true believer who got caught up in the moment, surrounded by dangerous influences and people who steered him further into a world he should never have been part of.
>
> I sincerely hope he reunites with his family, finds purpose, and uses the lessons he's learned to do something meaningful with his life. Having personally experienced

unjust detention, I can empathize with what he and his family have endured. While I may not believe in Ross's innocence, I hope the time he spent in prison has helped him understand the value of life and family and given him a new perspective moving forward.

Of course, Ulbricht left behind a legacy bigger than his jail cell. The blueprint he pioneered gave birth to countless dark-web successors, trading everything from hacked credit cards to human organs, a legacy of e-commerce that Jeff Bezos only wishes he could match.

The timing of Ulbricht's release was convenient when it came to cryptocurrency as well—Trump's cryptocurrency donors had been getting nervous about all that regulation talk, and here was a grand gesture to reassure them that the real criminals weren't the ones funneling Bitcoin into the ether, but the government bureaucrats trying to stop them. The crypto market surged: nothing says "regulatory green light" like a presidential pardon for the most infamous dark-web mogul of all time. Bitcoin investors popped champagne, while financial regulators considered early retirement.

What will Bitcoin be worth when you read this? I couldn't venture to guess how much higher the market cap of Bitcoin (or any cryptocurrency, for that matter) will rise, or how massively it will fall. Nobody knows the future. If they did, they could make a killing in online betting. I wouldn't have bet on Mark Karpelès ever being found innocent.

There was a lottery to get a seat in the courtroom on March 15, 2019, the day that the verdict for Mark Karpelès was handed down.

I didn't win the lottery, but Mark did. On two counts. I did not expect to win, but neither did I expect Karpelès to walk out with a not-guilty verdict on two out of three charges in a system where the accused has a less than 1 percent chance of winning. And I wasn't too upset about my own unlucky draw; Nathalie Stucky managed to get into the courtroom, proving that sometimes the odds are on your side. It was a Friday when it happened, and a very Good Friday indeed.

In December 2018, as you might remember, the prosecutors had asked for Mark to be punished with ten years in jail. It had already been over five years since his company and his life had collapsed. Now, the panel of judges found him innocent of the major charges of embezzlement and breach of trust. They found him guilty of improper management of electronic funds—but gave him a suspended sentence of four years.

A suspended sentence in Japan is a very good thing. In simple terms, if Karpelès kept his nose clean and didn't break the law, he would not go back to jail and would remain a free man. Four years have since passed. He's in the clear.

One of the presiding judges pointed out that none of the charges against Karpelès had anything to do with the missing bitcoins, and that Karpelès had never intended to harm the company or embezzle funds. His sole crime stemmed from installing a program in the system that tried to recoup the missing bitcoins that the firm had been saddled with from the time he took it over in March 2011.

The same judge admonished the prosecution for essentially mounting a frivolous case on the alleged embezzlement charges, "in which there was no intention to break the law and no laws broken." One of the panel of judges also mentioned the arrest of Alexander Vinnik, implying that the Tokyo police and prosecutors had failed in their original investigation. He seemed to suggest that the police had arrested Karpelès in an attempt to make him confess to a crime that they could not solve.

Kim Nilsson felt that the suspended sentence and partial-guilty verdict was fair, but that the other charges were bogus. In a way, the court condemned Karpelès for what has long been his critical fault—a failure to understand that not all things broken can be fixed. There are many quirky things about him, but perhaps the oddest is that he seems to have taken many years to realize that the world, human relationships, and deeds can't be dismantled and reassembled like a toy radio.

I had made arrangements with Karpelès to get his comment after the trial, and by this time I was just calling him Mark. The distance that I tried to keep in my head and in my terms of address had faded somewhere among the years of working on this story.

He texted me back his thoughts:

> Thanks for everything. I am grateful to the court and happy to be judged not guilty for embezzlement and breach of trust. I will discuss with my lawyers and decide how to proceed on the remaining charge. I knew it is very unlikely for the court to reach a not guilty verdict. That's very unusual in Japan. I am grateful to my lawyer and everyone who supported me.

The coverage of the trial was muted and odd. Some Japanese newspapers ran articles with "Karpelès Found Innocent On Two Charges" as the headline; others ran with "Karpelès Found Guilty" in the headline, and casually mentioned that he had been found not guilty of the major charges.

Most of the Japanese press deliberately failed to mention Vinnik, and simply referred to the hacking of Mt. Gox as being unsolved and to the case as technically closed. The sins of omission were understandable. Prosecutors in Japan hand-feed scoops to the mainstream press, and lapdogs don't like to bite the hands that feed them. And, as we have seen in the Carlos Ghosn case, the prosecutors retaliate with vicious vigor when challenged or made to lose face.

Speaking of Carlos Ghosn, by the way, partially by my introduction, he and Karpelès became nominal friends—I gave Ghosn a copy of this early draft of the book, in French, when I met him in July 2019. They have a lot in common, but I didn't even know they were friends until after Ghosn made his daring escape on December 29, 2019, leaving what would have been a never-ending legal limbo in Japan for the relative safety of Lebanon.

Karpelès was surprised, and surprisingly not that supportive of Ghosn's decision. When I asked him what he thought of "The Great Escape", shortly afterwards, he had this to say:

> I think that although the odds were against him, and even though he would never be found not guilty on all charges—the prosecutors have to save face, you know—he might have been found innocent on some charges. Look at me—I stayed and I fought and I won, mostly.

He should have stayed and sought justice. And then, when they found him guilty, it would still not have been too late to escape.

The Japanese prosecutors, were of course, publicly outraged, and when Ghosn held a press conference in Beirut on January 8, 2020, berating Japan's hostage justice system, the justice minister, Ms. Masako Mori, held a midnight press conference to respond to Ghosn's claims that Japan's justice system was unfair, brutal, and inhumane—as we know it is.

Mori aimed to convince the world that Japan had an equitable judicial system, in line with its status as a G3 nation. But among her many remarks accusing Ghosn of propagating lies about Japan, she put her high-heeled foot in her mouth.

"If he's clean as he says he is, then he should fairly and squarely prove his innocence in the court of law," she said. She subsequently posted her remark on social media. The backlash was not swift, but it was severe.

Former special prosecutor Nobou Gohara, a vocal critic of the Ghosn investigation and of Tokyo prosecutors, did not mince his words.

He commented, "The prosecutor has to establish guilt; to say the accused has to prove they are innocent is absolute bullshit. Even though the minister is a lawyer, she clearly has no understanding that 'presumed innocent until proven guilty' is a fundamental, basic principle."

A French lawyer, Francois Zimeray, retained by Ghosn, was also quick to point out the error. "It belongs to the prosecution to prove guilt and not to the accused person to prove innocence," he stated.

Legal theory has never won mass public interest in Japan, but after the Mori affair, "proof of innocence" (*muzai shomei*) was trending on Twitter.

Netizens pointed out: "She just admitted that what Ghosn was saying is true." Comments on social media included, "If the Minister of Justice doesn't understand that the prosecutors have to prove guilt or the accused is innocent, well of course [Ghosn] is going to want to escape. Is this a witch hunt from the Middle Ages?"

The answer is, yes. When accused in Japan, you are treated like a witch. If you're innocent, you drown; if you're guilty, you swim, and then are executed. Either way, you're dead once you're accused—usually figuratively, of course.

The world is full of injustice. And, to our surprise, Special Agent Tigran Gambaryan ended up on the receiving end of a gross miscarriage of justice.

The Bitcoin case was one of the last cases Tigran worked on at the IRS before pivoting to private industry. The book *Tracers in the Dark* by Andy Greenberg tells the story of his heroic work, along with other special agents, in investigating cybercrimes such as ransomware and the distribution of child pornography. Tigran is still involved with cryptocurrency, and is working as a compliance officer at Binance, a massive cryptocurrency-exchange platform. His work and life were suddenly upended, however, when he was illegally incarcerated in Nigeria in early 2024.

Following the collapse of its currency, the naira, the Nigerian government accused Binance of tax evasion and money laundering. They invited Tigran to come to the country in February 2024 to discuss their concerns, but upon his arrival he was promptly arrested on bogus charges and held without bail. In the eight months he was held captive, he contracted malaria, pneumonia, and tonsillitis. He had a concerning, persistent chest infection, and a back injury so severe it required surgery. He was denied mobility devices and medical care. He was also denied contact with his legal team. He was effectively being held hostage until they thought they could get Binance to pay his ransom. (This is, by the way, the unjust detention he alluded to when talking about Ulbricht.) Binance didn't pay a ransom.

And then, in October 2024, after much pressure from the United States, all the way up to the president himself, Nigeria dropped its charges against him; he was released. He is now a free man, and recovering from the spinal surgery needed after his months in captivity.

And on the topic of happy endings—and not the kind that Mark used to pay for—we have one for you.

Remember Dorian Nakamoto? He was not the real Satoshi. *Newsweek* ran their scoop, but, of course, it didn't take long for things to unravel. Nakamoto denied everything, and it became increasingly clear that he wasn't the enigmatic genius behind Bitcoin. He was simply a man in the wrong place at the wrong time, with an unfortunate overlap in name.

But the damage had been done. Reporters camped outside his home, his privacy was shattered, and Nakamoto—a man who valued nothing more than his peace and quiet—was caught in a maelstrom of attention he never asked for. It was a story that left a bad taste in the mouths of many, especially in the Bitcoin community, which valued privacy almost as much as it valued profits.

And that's when something unexpected happened. Andreas Antonopoulos, a prominent figure in the Bitcoin community, stepped up to the plate. He initiated a crowdfunding effort on Nakamoto's behalf. "If this person is Satoshi," he said, "the funds are a small 'thanks,' and won't make much of a difference. However, if this person is not Satoshi, then these funds will serve as a 'sorry for what happened to you'". It was a gesture of goodwill, and it struck a chord.

In the end, the community raised nearly sixty-seven bitcoins for Nakamoto, which, at the time, amounted to a value of around $23,000. It was an attempt at restitution—a small way of saying "our bad" for the colossal misunderstanding. By December 2017, Nakamoto had reportedly cashed out most of his holdings, earning himself an estimated $273,000. For someone who had been thrust into the limelight against his will, it was perhaps the best possible outcome.

In a story filled with the kind of people you'd expect to find in a true-crime podcast—hackers, opportunists, mysterious pseudonyms—Dorian Nakamoto stood out as the reluctant everyman. He wasn't interested in cryptocurrency or in being a part of the narrative. He simply wanted his quiet life back, and thanks to a community that recognized its mistake, he got at least some compensation for the ordeal.

Whether or not Nakamoto found comfort in the Bitcoin windfall is anyone's guess, but one hopes he took solace in the kindness shown to him after the chaos. Sometimes, even in the murky waters of the internet and those blinded by their love of bitcoin, there's a glimmer of humanity.

In the spirit of Christmas, I find myself reflecting on Satoshi Nakamoto, the mysterious creator of Bitcoin. We still don't know who he—or she—really is, but we do know one thing: they never wanted the spotlight. Satoshi has remained a ghost, a phantom, all while Bitcoin continues to surge, crash, rise, and repeat.

And here we are, in 2025, with the value of one bitcoin now hovering around $100,000. I've long since sold my own modest holdings, leaving the dreams of crypto riches to those who have the patience to ride the waves. I'm unable to surf; I can barely stand on a paddleboard.

In what seems like just another in the slew of unending updates to this book, Alexander Vinnik, one of the masterminds behind the hack of Mt. Gox, was abruptly traded to his home country, Russia, on February 12, 2025. This was a deal brokered by the governments of—who else?—Donald Trump and Vladmir Putin, despite a general agreement by most world leaders to isolate the latter following Russia's invasion of Ukraine.

Reuters, reporting on the swap, in an article titled, "Who is Alexander Vinnik, the Russian prisoner being traded for American Marc Fogel?" noted:

> Andrei Zakharov, a journalist who has written a book on Vinnik, said the Russian was reputed to control 80,000 bitcoins stolen from Mt. Gox in 2011, giving Moscow a strong interest in his return.
>
> "80 thousand bitcoins. 8 billion dollars. 2% of federal budget revenues for 2025. Welcome home!" he posted on Telegram.

The Devil takes Bitcoin. And so does Putin. It's like a horrific version of the famous James Bond novel in which the evil villain wins: *To Russia With Love*.

Contrary to Reuters' report, Vinnik only seems to have stolen 60,000 bitcoins, but $6 billion, well, that's still a nice chunk of change.

And what a deal it was to trade Vinnik in exchange for Marc Fogel, who had been sentenced to fourteen years in Russian prison for "drug smuggling." (In fact, it was for possessing medically prescribed marijuana.) It is commendable that Fogel has been returned home, particularly because his crime was so small. Russian news sources seemed to agree on this point, hardly mentioning Fogel in their coverage of the swap. However, what was concerning about this exchange was the tacit acceptance of the notion that Vinnik's crimes were similarly small.

Dmitry Peskov, press secretary for Putin, was quoted in *Russia Today* on February 14, 2025 as saying, "For all of us and, of course also, for the president of Russia, it's always a joy when a citizen of Russia, who served a completely unjustified punishment in the US, returns from there to their motherland."

Vinnik arrived back in the motherland on Valentine's Day. According to the state-owned news agency TASS, and other sources, the Russian Ministry of Internal Affairs began investigating Vinnik in 2017 for large-scale fraud, computer crimes, and embezzlement, and suspected that he had misappropriated over 600,000 rubles. Absent in the Russian media reports were any direct mentions of BTC-e, the platform that Vinnik created and used to facilitate drug trafficking, personal data theft, and money laundering to the tune of billions of dollars in bitcoins stolen from Mt. Gox—a hacking he orchestrated.

However, the nature of these charges—minor in comparison to the multi-billion-dollar money-laundering accusations he faced in the US and Europe—suggests that Russia's interest in Vinnik may have been more about securing his return than prosecuting him. This aligns with reports that BTC-e's assets were ultimately taken over by Konstantin Malofeev, a businessman with ties to Russia's FSB.

The FSB (Federal Security Service of the Russian Federation) is Russia's primary domestic intelligence and security agency. It is the successor to the KGB's internal security functions and is responsible for counterintelligence, counterterrorism, border security, and surveillance of perceived threats to the state.

The FSB operates under the direct control of the president of Russia, giving it significant power in domestic affairs, cyber operations, and intelligence gathering. It has been linked to high-profile political repression, cyber warfare, and covert influence operations both inside and outside Russia. Given its deep ties to oligarchs and state-controlled enterprises, suspicions that BTC-e's assets ended up under the control of Malofeev—an oligarch linked to the FSB, a close friend of Putin, and a co-founder of the international investment fund Marshall Capital Partners—suggest that the Russian authorities may have had a strategic interest in the cryptocurrency exchange, rather than treating Vinnik as a criminal suspect.

"Instead of a genuine crackdown, the Russian investigation was probably a pretext to bring him back under

Russian control, ensuring that any knowledge he had about BTC-e's financial flows remained within Moscow's orbit," one IRS investigator familiar with the case told us.

Vinnik's defense was always that he was just a technical specialist, not directly involved in any crimes. TASS reported that the Ministry of Internal Affairs has taken Vinnik off the wanted list, citing a lack of evidence for their 2017 investigation.

Suffice it to say, it is largely believed that he will not be completing the third of his world tour of consecutive sentences—a dangerous concession, if not endorsement, by the government of the United States.

After the deal was made, Tigran Gambaryan, the former special agent who had put him away, posted a picture on LinkedIn of himself in the office when he was working the case, and wrote:

> I took this photo in the early hours of July 25, 2017, while coordinating between agents from IRS-CI, FBI, USSS, HSI, and FDIC during the arrest of Alexander Vinnik in Greece and simultaneous operations in the U.S. This marked the culmination of years of collaboration between NDCA and my partners at FBI Louisville, USSS Washington D.C., HSI San Francisco, and FDIC Washington DC.
>
> Today, it was announced that Vinnik was part of a prisoner swap that secured the release of Marc Fogel. I want to give a shout out to the many friends and colleagues who played a role in the investigation and to congratulate Fogel and his family on finally putting this nightmare behind them. I also hope Vinnik can use this opportunity to turn his life around and do something positive.

This was one of the most intense investigations I've ever been part of—but also one of the best examples of interagency collaboration I witnessed in the U.S. government. No egos, just dedication. Nothing can take away from what we accomplished.

Mark Karpelès, over the phone, had only a few words to say. "I spent a year in jail for crimes I didn't commit, and the man who victimized me, ripped off our customers, and ruined the lives of thousands just walked away scott-free and probably with thousands of bitcoins. Is this American justice?"

"Yep, Mark," I told him." That's American justice. Always for sale. Trump's America isn't a country, it's just a grift."

Finally, a few final words about Mark Karpelès. He's still here, and he's even published a book: *Cryptocurrency 3.0*. It's about the promise of digital currencies and their dark side. Mark is enjoying the perks of being that rarest of things—a man found innocent at trial in Japan. In September 2024, he launched a new cryptocurrency exchange in Europe. He is trying to launch it in Japan, but faces a very long uphill battle. Yet he remains undaunted if you ask him about it.

"Should be fine."

In 2025, he plans to open a non-profit organization, UNGOX, which will give ratings to cryptocurrency exchanges—like Moody's or the S&P, minus the financial crisis. The world could surely use some unbiased indicators of which exchanges are legit and which are bogus. Mark may not be rich anymore, but he's free. And that, dear reader, is worth more than all the bitcoins in the world.

Many of those who lost the money and bitcoins they entrusted to Mt. Gox and Mark are now being paid back. The trustee is making the payments.

I realized a few weeks ago that I *still* had one bitcoin sitting in an account in the United States. I had completely forgotten about it, but in the process of revising this manuscript with Amy Plambeck, I checked to see if it was still there—or, rather, if the Bitcoin exchange I had stored it in was still in business. Happy to say, I wasn't 'Goxxed'.

Over the years, as I have watched the price of Bitcoin surge and fall, I have lost most of the interest I ever had in cryptocurrency. I realize that some people have become very wealthy trading in virtual currencies, and sometimes I really wish I had followed in their footsteps. There is a certain amount of nirvana of having money in the bank, but probably more nirvana when it's fiat currency. But I can't quite convince myself to cash out. I still have a wallet.

And I still haven't changed my Twitter (aka X) handle. If you look, I'm still claiming to be Satoshi Nakamoto. I fear once I change that handle, I'll lose it forever. And there's something quite fun about making some people wonder. I'm sure the real Satoshi Nakamoto, sitting on billions of dollars of bitcoin, if they are alive, doesn't mind. Maybe he can spare a few BTC for me, too.

If you'd like to donate some bitcoins to a good cause—namely, me and my writing partners—I wouldn't stop you. Just check the wallet below. If the devil takes payments in Bitcoin, I guess I'm willing to take it as well:

3LQpbUvDrJTuKEtMg375VsQkEN5X59PYvg

Acknowledgments

This is the part of the book where I thank all the people who helped make it possible, and no one deserves more credit and more thanks that Nathalie Kyoko Stucky aka Kyoko Miura (三浦郷子) whose name was cleverly hidden on the original front cover in kanji next to my Zen Buddhist priest name (和洲良舒). She did the majority of the groundwork, and this book wouldn't have been possible without her. Nathalie is busy these days raising a lovely little child, Lisa, in Switzerland. Nathalie has reported on Bitcoin extensively over the years—much more than I have. The main reason my name is on the cover is that I had the time to take our original work and revisit it, update it, and put it together in a book that hopefully is both a good introduction to Bitcoin, the criminals, entrepreneurs, and true believers that have flocked to it, and the final word on a real-life mystery. My kids are both in college now and require less attention; raising little Lisa is a full-time job.

You may have heard of "a captive audience," but this book had a "captive editor." Special thanks to former Special Agent Tigran Gambaryan, who read an early draft of the manuscript and provided valuable advice from the dens of a Nigerian prison while unjustly detained. During his time in captivity, he managed to smuggle a cell phone into his cell—never has the term 'cell phone' been more correct—and I wrote to him almost every day. I wish I could say I wrote to my mother that often, because I would be the ideal Jewish boy, but that is not the case. Sorry, Mom. It is with great delight that I am writing this up, knowing that he is out of jail and recovering.

Special thanks should also go to Amy Plambeck, who helped update and rewrite this book in English. As always, I bow deeply in the direction of Henry Rosenbloom, the founder of Scribe, who also edited this manuscript. There are very few publishers in this world who also double as ace editors. Ten thousand thanks.

I am grateful to Julianne Chiaet, who was a copyeditor on an earlier version of this book, and also the main English translation editor of *Le Dernier des yakuzas*, available from Scribe as *The Last Yakuza*, also deserves kudos. I wish to thank Lauren Hardie, who copyedited the original *Daily Beast* articles and Silk Road chapter. I am also very grateful to Mari Yamamoto, my best friend and fellow journalist, who often picked up the slack while I was working on this book and covering other stories. I don't think that I could have finished it without her tangible and intangible support.

Thank you to Christopher Dickey, the foreign editor at *The Daily Beast*, who supported our reporting on this story, as well as John Avlon, Katie Baker, and Noah Shachtman, who were also at *The Daily Beast*. Chris passed away in 2020 during the pandemic. He is greatly missed.

I would also like to thank a few very special agents and cops of good conscience who were willing to share intelligence with me, perhaps when it was not always in their best interests. Thanks to Mark Karpelès and his lawyer, Nobuyasu Ogata, for their patience with my many questions. Thanks to Kim Nilsson for his time and help as well. I feel I must also nod in thanks to Bitcoin Jesus, aka Roger Ver, who not only answered many of our questions, but somewhere along the line also gave me a free bitcoin cap and has given writing work to Ms. Stucky in the past. I hope he gets out of jail by the time this book is in print.

Of course, I would like to thank the team at Marchialy, who convinced me to write the book for a French audience in the first place. Clémence, our editor-in-chief, painstakingly went through the book line-by-line, checking dates and editing for clarity. Her suggestions on how to make the book better were fundamentally correct, and I'm glad I followed her lead. The cover artwork by Guillaume was just amazing, as all are his covers. And I want to make a deep, on-the-knees bow of gratitude to my French-language translator, Cyril Gay. He is not just a translator; he is a writer of great talent and my French muse. When you see his name on a book, you should take that as a sign you're about to read something excellent.

I would like to thank you, the reader, for buying or borrowing this book. If you were expecting a tome about the Japanese underworld, I'm sorry if I disappointed you. There actually have been some yakuza involved in the Bitcoin boom in Japan, including members of the Yamaguchi-gumi

Kodo-kai, but I'll save those stories for another book and another time. I hope that the book proved to be edifying and entertaining, and if it was both, I will feel very content.

Finally, thanks to Satoshi Nakamoto, wherever you are. I have only bought two bitcoins in my life, but I made $10,000 out of the deal, which paid for my daughter's first year of college. So ... thank you!